GUILT-FREE
SNACKS

This book is dedicated to those who strive to thrive. Those who wake up every day and make the conscious choice to eat better, feel better, think better and do better – not only for themselves, but for those around them and for the planet.

SWEET & SAVOURY BITES TO POWER YOU THROUGH THE DAY

GUILT-FREE
SNACKS

LUKE HINES

  Pan Macmillan Australia

CONTENTS

INTRODUCTION

Hi, I'm Luke and I'm a snackaholic. That's right, I said it, I own it and I love it! I love making snacks and I love eating snacks. And if you don't already, you will too after getting stuck into all the delicious recipes I have jam-packed into this bigger than bite-sized cookbook.

Those of you who've followed my cooking journey so far – on television and social media and in books – know I love creating snacks. And not just any type of snack: real-deal, nutrient-dense, actually good-for-you healthy snacks. But with one caveat: they must never be boring or bland. I've always believed that if you're going to eat better and look after your health, it should be absolutely, categorically moreish and delicious, and that's where this book comes in.

By definition, a snack is something small you eat between larger meals. But snacking itself often gets a bad rap because people associate snacks with processed and refined convenience foods that can have a negative effect on your health. When you snack smart, snacks can actually support your health and wellness journey, improve your wellbeing and keep you on track.

I've written *Guilt-free Snacks* to give you guys the ultimate companion to sweet and savoury snacks for any occasion. You can enjoy these snacks between meals or as meal replacements when you're short on time and big on hunger. I've got you covered for any time of day, with hungry-thirsty quenching smoothies, juices and shots that are as quick to make as they are delicious. You'll be on a roll with my massive array of bliss-ball bites that pack just as much flavour as they do health benefits. Workouts will never be the same once you try my pre- and post-exercise treats, tried and tested by me for optimal performance and recovery. You'll be the talk of the town the next time you host drinks and nibbles because I've dedicated an entire chapter to chips, crisps and dips. And your kitchen will smell like an absolute delight when you whip up the warm and toasty recipes from the baking chapter. I'm famous for my healthy versions of well-known treats and favourite takeaways and fast foods, and this book doesn't disappoint on recipes that are just like the real thing. Plus, comfort food has never looked or tasted so good, with an entire chapter dedicated to indulgent treats and mouth-watering midnight snacks.

Continued overleaf >>

As with all my cookbooks, I've got all your allergens covered with a handy reference guide and key for each recipe so you know exactly what you're getting and what simple swaps you can make to adapt it to suit your diet or lifestyle. As a starting point, you'll find all my recipes are gluten and refined-sugar free, with minimal dairy that can be easily swapped out if needed. From plant-based vegan to low-carb keto, there is something here for everyone. Remember: there is no one-size-fits-all approach to what you can or can't eat, just listen to your body and do what works for you.

Guilt-free Snacks is all about proving you *can* have your cake and eat it too. And by that, I mean you can still snack your little heart out without throwing any health, diet or lifestyle goals out the window. In fact, I wrote this book to enhance your health journey, with each and every bite. This book is simple: really good, honest recipes loaded with real-food ingredients that actually taste great and are genuinely good for you. Get in the kitchen, get cooking and, most of all, have fun.

Luke xx

INTRODUCTION

WHY SNACK?

Did I mention I love snacking? It's like a mini opportunity for me to enjoy the spoils of good food between larger meals. I'm both a mentally and physically active person and, if I'm not fasting, I find snacking is a really great way to stay energised and focused throughout the day. For me, there is nothing more distracting than feeling ravenously hungry. When I get overly hungry, I can't concentrate, become agitated and both my physical and mental performance decline until I satisfy my cravings. But the key is *how* I refuel. And that's where *Guilt-free Snacks* comes in handy.

These are optimal recipes that will refuel your body, increase physical energy, improve mental focus and satiate your appetite, keeping you feeling fuller for longer. When you fill up on wholesome, nutrient-dense ingredients, there's no room for inflammatory, processed and refined foods that can be detrimental to your health. There's only so much we can eat in a day, so every meal choice, and importantly every snack we enjoy, is an opportunity to fill your day's 'fuel' tank with all things good. When your car has run out of petrol, you don't fill half the tank with petrol and half with water in an attempt to save time or money – your car would break down and you'd have serious engine issues. We are the same. You shouldn't fill half your tank with health food and half with junk, because very soon you will look, feel and perform poorly, and begin to have long-term digestive, weight or inflammatory issues.

Every mouthful you take each day is a chance to better your health. And that's why snacking smart is so important.

LESS ROOM FOR CRAP

Being prepared by having a stash of healthy snacks on hand will help prevent you from reaching for, craving or needing snacks that aren't good for you. The more you fill up on good, the less room you have for bad.

YOU ARE HUNGRY

It's okay to be hungry between meals. You won't always feel satisfied hunger-wise or nutritionally from your larger main meals, so don't be afraid to fill in these gaps with nutrient-dense snacks.

YOU REQUIRE MORE NUTRIENTS

Everything from increased exercise, mental stimulation or incidental activity to hormonal changes, breastfeeding or medical conditions can result in us needing to snack. Sometimes your body just needs more food, more often.

IT WORKS FOR YOU

Some people thrive by enjoying two larger meals a day and fasting, others love three big meals per day with no snacks, but a lot of people love smaller, more regular meals and snacks. There is no right answer and you and your lifestyle determine what's right for you. Wanna snack? Then snack!

YOU NOTORIOUSLY MIDNIGHT SNACK

I've been there, trust me. I've focused on eating really well all day, and restricted my food intake, then come to after-dinner time and I am ready to devour the entire pantry and fridge. What starts as a small dessert turns into the entire packet of something – or three! Prevent the night-time binge with a more balanced intake of food with snacks throughout the day.

YOU LACK ENERGY

If you're someone who struggles with low blood-sugar levels and you begin to fade or feel hungry throughout the day, then snacking could be just the answer to give you more energy and focus.

YOU WANT TO

Sometimes there doesn't have to be a reason beyond you simply want to. You like to snack, you love making snacks, you enjoy it, then do it. You do you, boo!

SNACK SMART

Not all snacks are created equal, and I think that's why for so long snacking got such a bad rap. Traditionally, snacking meant something from a packet that was highly processed and refined, and most likely laden with sugars, seed oils and fillers I can't even pronounce. So, knowing how to snack smart can make a huge difference to your health and wellness journey. And here's how.

FAIL TO PREPARE OR PREPARE TO FAIL

I love this saying. When it comes to snacking, it basically means that if you don't spend some quality time preparing healthy snacks in advance, you are likely to get caught out and have no other choice but to reach for a less-than-ideal convenience snack with who knows what in it. So, prepare ahead and give yourself time to choose your snack recipes for the week. Get to the shops to load up on the ingredients you need, then make your creations so you have snacks on hand for when those cravings kick in.

BULK BATCH MAKE AND BAKE

Once you've made time for what you want to make, I recommend preparing one or multiple snacks in bulk. Enjoy some on the day, then store some in the fridge and some in the freezer for the days, weeks or months ahead. You can never have too many pre-made snacks on hand for when you're short on time but big on hunger.

WHAT FOR WHEN

Knowing what you want to snack on and for when is important. A pre-workout snack will be different to what you want post-workout, much like how an on the way to work morning snack will be different to a pre-bed midnight snack. Know what you need energy-wise and choose recipes based on that requirement so you're satisfying the craving and energy needs for each occasion.

MAYBE YOU'RE JUST THIRSTY

Dehydration often presents itself as hunger, so make sure you stay adequately hydrated throughout the day. Aim for a minimum of 2 litres of fluid per day, but don't forget to take into account the need for extra to counterbalance diuretic drinks such as coffee, or water lost from exercise and sweating.

KNOW WHAT CONSTITUTES A GOOD SNACK

The best type of snack is one that you make from scratch. Realistically, however, we can't always have it that way. Lean towards snacks that are gluten free, refined-sugar free, lower carb and high in healthy fats, made from unrefined, unprocessed ingredients from high-welfare animals and local, organic produce, if possible. Knowing where our food was grown, caught, raised and produced and how it was transported enables us to make better choices for the sake of our own health and that of the planet.

KNOW YOUR LABELS

You won't always be in a position to have my snacktastic creations on hand, and knowing what to look for on labels can be a massive help for when you're on the go. When choosing any pre-made or store-bought snacks, my rule of thumb is: less than 5 grams of sugar per serve, free from any artificial ingredients, no refined seed oils (such as canola or sunflower), gluten and refined-sugar free. Look for a decent hit of fibre, well-sourced protein, slower burning carbs and quality healthy fats.

SAY NO

Understanding when to say no to snacks is equally as important as knowing when to snack. Sometimes we snack out of pure boredom, for emotional reasons, or simply because we are offered one. Learn to say no to mindless snacking without any purpose. If you're not genuinely hungry, don't know what's in it, or are simply having it for the sake of it, that's when snacking isn't ideal. Say no.

FIND THAT BALANCE

If in doubt, find a balance between the three core snack ingredients: well-sourced protein from plants or animals, good-quality healthy fats and unrefined carbs from whole foods. Protein helps keep you feeling fuller for longer and repairs and rebuilds muscles. Healthy fats can balance hormones, keep our energy levels stable and improve our mood, and well-sourced smart carbs can provide superior sources of energy for overall performance, repair and function. Look for snacks that celebrate these three, or slide the scale accordingly. Reduce the carbs if you need a lower carb option, increase the protein post-workout, or up the fats to aid in fasting. Find *your* balance.

SNACKTASTIC HACKS

Most of us lead busy lives and are trying to stick to a budget. These are some of my best time- and money-saving tips.

CREATE A SNACK DAY

This is the day where you prep, plan, shop and make your snacks for the days, weeks or months ahead. Make a really fun day out of heading to the markets, finding awesome produce, pumping some tunes in the kitchen, then store as required to have snacks on hand anytime, anywhere.

DO IT TOGETHER

Make snacking more fun and varied by creating a snack circle with friends. You can each choose a different type of snack to make in bulk, then whip up a massive batch of it to portion out at a snack meet – aka school drop-off or gym class. You'll then have three or four different snacks to enjoy.

STORAGE KING OR QUEEN

Become the storage king or queen with a decent collection of resealable glass containers and reusable zip-lock bags. Having these on hand is perfect for when it comes time to portion up your snacks for proper storage. Storing snacks properly helps them last longer and go further.

DOUBLE IT

Got a favourite snack recipe in this book? Double or triple the quantities so you have extra. Preparing in bulk, you'll spend the same time making it but have a lot more to show for it. Plus, buying the ingredients in bulk can be much cheaper.

BUY IN BULK

When you know you're going to use a lot of a certain type of ingredient, buy it in bulk to save on the overall cost. Products like almond meal, nut butters and oils are always cheaper when purchased in larger quantities. So, although the upfront investment is slightly more, it's way better value and stocking up means you'll always have what you need to hand.

USE WHAT YOU HAVE FIRST

I'm guilty of heading to the local shop to buy new ingredients before using what I already have in the fridge and pantry. You'd be amazed how creative you can get by finishing off the leftovers lurking in the back of the fridge or on the pantry shelves. My recipes are really flexible and enable you to swap certain ingredients in and out, meaning there's no excuse not to use what you've got. My 'build your own' sections in each chapter are a game changer for this.

LAST LEGS

Fruit and veggies on their last legs at the shops are often less than half price, even when they're still perfectly good. When buying fresh food, don't be afraid to choose produce that is overripe, on its way out or looking a little worse for wear. Simply chop it up that day and freeze it to use in smoothies and smoothie bowls. Everything tastes the same once blitzed and blended into your favourite recipe.

RECIPE LEGEND

You'll see the following symbols next to each recipe to denote what category it falls into nutritionally. If the symbol has an asterisk, the recipe can be tweaked slightly with a simple swap to make it that way – just read the intro, ingredients or the snackable fact on how it can be done.

DF – DAIRY FREE

My recipes are 100 per cent lactose free and predominantly dairy free. Dairy and dairy products are derived from milk from mammals, mainly cows, sheep and goats. Some people can have an inflammatory response to dairy; in particular lactose, a sugar found in dairy. I've made this book safe for those of you who are lactose intolerant or simply don't enjoy high amounts of dairy, with the occasional exception of grass-fed butter, which is made from milk fat and protein and contains negligible traces of lactose. To make a recipe containing grass-fed butter 100 per cent dairy free, swap in the same quantity of extra-virgin coconut oil. If you choose to eat dairy, always make sure it's full fat, high welfare and, if possible, organic.

GF – GLUTEN FREE

All recipes in this book are free from ingredients containing gluten. Gluten is a protein found in certain grains that can cause an inflammatory response in some people. I choose to omit it from my recipes, making them safe for those who are sensitive, allergic, intolerant or simply wish to avoid it.

GF* A note on making recipes gluten free

Recipes in this book marked GF* call for rolled oats labelled as gluten free (or wheat free). Pure oats are gluten free; often it is the machinery they are processed with that contaminates them. If using, please always select certified gluten-free (or wheat-free) rolled oats to avoid cross-contamination from processing. Gluten-free rolled oats are suitable for those who choose to avoid products containing gluten but do not have any specific health issue; if, however, you are in any way sensitive, intolerant or allergic to gluten, especially if you have coeliac disease, only consume oats under the advice, support and guidance of your health professional, as avenin, the protein in oats, can cause inflammation and long-term damage.

LC – LOW CARB

A lot of my recipes are low carb and avoid higher carb starchy ingredients. Good examples include the use of almond meal instead of arrowroot or tapioca flour, above-ground vegetables instead of below-ground starchy varieties, and low-fructose berries instead of sweeter fruit options. When it comes to adding sweeteners, to make any recipe lower carb and/or keto friendly, I recommend using monk fruit sweeteners.

LC* A note on making recipes low carb/keto friendly

Recipes marked LC* can be made low carb/keto friendly by using monk fruit sweeteners. These come in both liquid and granule form, with a variety of different flavour profiles. I like Lakanto brand. In this book, if a recipe calls for monk fruit syrup, I recommend the Lakanto maple-flavoured syrup or golden malt-flavoured syrup. If a recipe calls for granulated monk fruit sweetener, or you'd like a low-carb keto swap for coconut sugar, I recommend the Lakanto classic, golden or baking blend varieties. They also make a low-carb alternative to icing sugar. These are all now readily available in supermarkets, health-food stores, online health retailers and my own online store.

NF – NUT FREE

Nuts can be an allergen or inflammatory food for some people, so I have given you a number of recipes that are, or can be, adapted to be nut free, making them suitable for school lunch boxes, too. If a recipe calls for nuts or nut butter and you'd like to make it nut free, simply swap for seeds and tahini.

PB – PLANT BASED

The majority of my recipes are plant based or can be adapted to be so. In this book, if a recipe is marked as plant based, it will be free from any animal products and is suitable for vegans and vegetarians. If a recipe calls for butter, it can be substituted with extra-virgin coconut oil, and if a recipe calls for eggs, they can in most cases be substituted with flax or chia eggs.

PB* A note on making recipes plant based

Recipes marked as PB* can be made plant based by swapping a free-range egg for a flax or chia egg. To make a flax or chia egg, combine 1 tablespoon of flaxseed or chia meal with 3 tablespoons of water in a small bowl, mix well and set aside for 5 minutes, or until thickened and ready to use.

SF – REFINED-SUGAR FREE

The recipes in this book are all refined-sugar free. All ingredients have natural sugars – even a low-carb vegetable like broccoli contains fructose, glucose, sucrose and tiny amounts of lactose and maltose – which means most recipes include sugar in some form, and we can't avoid it completely. We can, however, choose not to add refined or processed sugar. The refined-sugar-free sweeteners I use in this book are pure maple syrup, raw honey and coconut nectar. I also use monk fruit sweeteners to make my recipes lower carb and/or keto friendly; please see LC above for more on this.

QUENCH IT!

YOUR PLACE FOR HUNGRY-THIRSTY

TO SNACK OR NOT TO SNACK

To snack or not to snack, that is the question! Three key factors come into play when working out whether we should snack or not: dehydration, boredom and hunger. If in doubt, before I snack, I have a tall glass of water and sit tight for 15 minutes or so. If that takes away my craving, then I know it was dehydration kicking in. If I still crave something, I make sure it isn't just because I'm bored. Sometimes long stints on the laptop or mindless scrolling on our phones can have us reaching for food we don't really need or want, purely to kill time or stave off boredom. If I tune into my intuitive self and ask honestly if I'm having the snack for the sake of it or as a distraction, and my answer is no, then, boom, turns out I am actually hungry. And if you're actually hungry, it's really good to snack. Snacking keeps you from bingeing later on, allows you to maintain your physical and mental focus, and gets you through the day's adventures.

QUENCH IT!

COOKIES AND CREAM MYLKSHAKE

DF GF LC* PB SF

This recipe is the low-carb keto-friendly equivalent of throwing a few scoops of ice cream and some Oreo biscuits into a blender. What more could you ask for? When it comes to the plant-based milk you choose as your base, opt for one that's free from added sugars or fillers or, even better, make your own. For a thicker shake, use canned coconut cream rather than milk as your base.

250 ml (1 cup) coconut milk, almond milk or macadamia nut milk, chilled
2 tablespoons canned coconut cream
2 tablespoons maple syrup, honey, or maple-flavoured monk fruit syrup for low carb
120 g (½ cup) frozen sliced banana
70 g (½ cup) ice cubes

COOKIE CRUMB
3 tablespoons blanched almond meal or hazelnut meal
1 tablespoon fine desiccated coconut
1 heaped tablespoon cacao powder
1 teaspoon cacao nibs
1 teaspoon vanilla bean paste or powder
1 tablespoon maple syrup, honey, or maple-flavoured monk fruit syrup for low carb
1 tablespoon butter, ghee or coconut oil

To make the cookie crumb, toast the almond or hazelnut meal and desiccated coconut in a frying pan over medium heat, stirring frequently with a spatula or spoon, until golden brown. Transfer to a bowl, add the remaining cookie crumb ingredients and mix well until you have a clumpy looking chocolate crumb. Cover and place in the fridge or freezer to firm up while you get started on the mylkshake.

Place the plant-based milk, coconut cream, sweetener, banana and ice cubes in a food processor or high-speed blender and blitz until well combined. Spoon one-third of the cookie crumb into the mylkshake to give it a lovely speckled look. Spoon another one-third of the cookie crumb into the bottom of a tall glass, pour over the mylkshake, then top with the remaining cookie crumb. Enjoy immediately, served chilled.

SERVES 1

SNACKABLE FACT

Replacing our favourite sweet treats with a healthier alternative is more sustainable and enjoyable than avoiding that food altogether. Simple swaps like this one can help keep us on track with our long-term goals.

CHOC–CHERRY DELIGHT

DF GF LC* NF PB SF

I think what makes a Cherry Ripe such a delight to eat is the perfect balance between the subtle sweetness of the cherries and the bitterness of the chocolate combined with that undeniable coconut texture. I've re-created that experience in this smoothie with the best ingredients you can get. Not only is this good for your health, it's good for your tastebuds, too.

125 ml (½ cup) canned coconut milk
70 g (½ cup) ice cubes
160 g (1 cup) frozen pitted cherries, plus extra 3 tablespoons, roughly chopped
1 tablespoon maple syrup, honey, or maple-flavoured monk fruit syrup for low carb
1 teaspoon vanilla bean paste or powder

3 tablespoons shredded coconut, plus extra 1 tablespoon to serve
3 tablespoons melted dark chocolate (80% cacao minimum or to make your own, see page 40)
1 tablespoon cacao nibs, to serve

Place the coconut milk, ice cubes, frozen pitted cherries, sweetener, vanilla and coconut in a food processor or high-speed blender and blitz until well combined.

Take a tall glass and pour the melted chocolate around the inside rim and down the sides, reserving a little for the top. Pour the smoothie into the glass, top with the roughly chopped cherries, the extra coconut and the cacao nibs and drizzle over the reserved melted chocolate. Serve immediately.

Serves 1

VERY GOOD GREENS

DF GF NF PB SF

If you're looking for a green smoothie that doesn't taste like the actual garden, then you've come to the right place. This has the perfect balance between fruit and veggies without being overly sweet or not sweet enough. For a thicker smoothie, go with the coconut cream option; for a thinner smoothie, go with the coconut water.

125 ml (½ cup) canned coconut cream
   or coconut water
120 g (½ cup) finely sliced frozen banana
70 g (½ cup) ice cubes
45 g (1 cup) baby spinach leaves

1 green apple, cored and diced
1 kiwifruit, peeled and diced
1 Lebanese cucumber, roughly diced
1 small handful of fresh mint leaves,
   reserve some to serve

Place all the ingredients in a food processor or high-speed blender and blitz until well combined. Pour into a tall glass and top with the reserved mint leaves. Serve chilled.

Serves 1

SNACKABLE FACT

Turns out our parents weren't wrong all those times they told us how important it was to eat our greens. They're packed with fibre, which promotes healthy gut bacteria; they're loaded with vitamin C, which can support our immunity and natural collagen production; and most are low in carbs, meaning they provide a nutrient-dense boost without the bloat.

QUENCH IT!

BUILD YOUR OWN

SMOOTHIE

I love smoothies; they're the perfect go-to snack. Here is your ultimate smoothie guide that will allow you to create your favourite flavour combination.

Follow the outline below and for each component feel free to use one element straight up or try a combo of a few to make your perfect blend.

When experimenting with different ingredients, it's important to be intuitive. If your smoothie is too thick, add more liquid of choice; if it's too runny, add more dry ingredients.

Depending on what combo you create, your smoothies can be DF, GF, LC, NF, PB or SF.

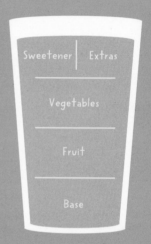

BASE
250 ml (1 cup)

almond milk
coconut milk
coconut water
filtered water
freshly squeezed fruit juice
hemp milk
ice cubes
macadamia nut milk

FRESH OR FROZEN FRUIT
1 cup sliced or chopped

apple
banana
blackberries
blueberries
kiwifruit
mango
pineapple
raspberries
strawberries
watermelon

QUENCH IT!

VEGETABLES
1 cup sliced or chopped

carrots
celery
cucumber
kale
spinach
Swiss chard

SWEETENER
to taste (optional)

coconut sugar
honey
maple syrup
monk fruit syrup
stevia

EXTRAS
to taste

avocado
bee pollen
cacao nibs
cacao powder
collagen powder
fresh or ground ginger
ground cinnamon
ground nutmeg
mint leaves
muesli or granola
nut butter
protein powder
vanilla bean paste
or powder

METHOD

Place your preferred combination of ingredients in a food processor or high-speed blender and blitz until well combined. Pour into a tall glass and enjoy immediately.

Serves 1

SALTED PEANUT BUTTER AND CARAMEL THICKSHAKE

DF GF NF* PB SF

When writing this book for you guys, I really wanted to make sure each and every recipe showcased the absolute best flavour combinations because when it comes to smoothies, life is too short for them to be boring, bland or the same every day. Peanut butter and caramel are an incredible combo, and a pinch of salt really takes this to the next level.

125 ml (½ cup) canned coconut milk
120 g (½ cup) thickly sliced frozen banana
70 g (½ cup) ice cubes
4 medjool dates, pitted and soaked in
    hot water for 15 minutes, drained

1 tablespoon maple syrup, coconut nectar
    or maple-flavoured monk fruit syrup
1 tablespoon natural crunchy peanut butter,
    plus extra to serve
pinch of sea salt
¼ teaspoon cacao powder, to sprinkle

Place the coconut milk, banana, ice cubes, dates, sweetener, peanut butter and salt in a food processor or high-speed blender and blitz until well combined. Pour into a tall glass, sprinkle over the cacao powder and drizzle on some extra peanut butter. Enjoy immediately.

Serves 1

SNACKABLE FACT

You can make this recipe nut free by swapping out the peanut butter for tahini. Tahini, a similar consistency paste made from ground sesame seeds, is equally as delicious in this thickshake.

FULLY LOADED CHOC–MINT BULLETPROOF COFFEE

DF GF LC* NF SF

By now you will have heard of the bulletproof-coffee phenomenon in the low carb, keto and fasting space. Not just for devotees of those lifestyles, bulletproof coffee is a fantastic choice for anyone wanting to supercharge their day. This combo is the perfect snack, meal replacement ... or just because. If you don't have any edible peppermint oil, simply omit it altogether and you'll have a plain chocolate version.

250 ml (1 cup) hot strong black coffee
1 tablespoon MCT oil (see page 62)
1 tablespoon unflavoured collagen powder
1 teaspoon butter or ghee

1 teaspoon maple syrup, or maple-flavoured monk fruit syrup for low carb
1 teaspoon cacao powder
2 drops edible essential peppermint oil

Place all the ingredients in a high-speed blender and blitz, starting on low speed and building up to medium, for 30–45 seconds until well combined and emulsified. Pour into a mug or heatproof glass and enjoy nice and hot.

Serves 1

TIP

Be mindful when blending hot ingredients – ensure the lid is secured and, for extra safety, hold a tea towel over the top in case any spills out at higher speeds.

STACKED
HOT CHOCCIE

DF GF LC* NF PB* SF

I have always loved a good hot chocolate. What if we could take that pared-back classic to the next level and turn the drink we love into a snack that will keep us going for longer? If you're looking for an extra kick in the morning, simply add a shot or two of espresso to make a hot chocolate coffee that will have you smiling all day.

250 ml (1 cup) canned coconut milk
1 tablespoon cacao powder
1 tablespoon maple syrup, coconut nectar, or maple-flavoured monk fruit syrup for low carb
1 tablespoon unflavoured collagen powder, or unflavoured plant-based protein powder for plant based

¼ teaspoon maca powder
¼ teaspoon ground cinnamon
2 tablespoons canned coconut cream
1 teaspoon cacao nibs

In a saucepan over high heat, warm the coconut milk until just boiled and starting to bubble.

Remove from the heat and stir through the cacao powder, sweetener, collagen or protein and maca powders and cinnamon. Whiz together using a high-speed blender, starting on low speed and building to medium, until thick, creamy and emulsified. Pour into a large mug, dollop on the coconut cream and sprinkle over the cacao nibs. Best enjoyed immediately.

Serves 1

SNACKABLE FACT

If you've got the time and ingredients on hand, try swapping the cacao powder for melted dark chocolate, around the 80 per cent cacao mark. Simply add the melted chocolate to the other ingredients in the blender and be blown away with how thick it makes your drink. If you've got any left over, drizzle some on top of your drink, too.

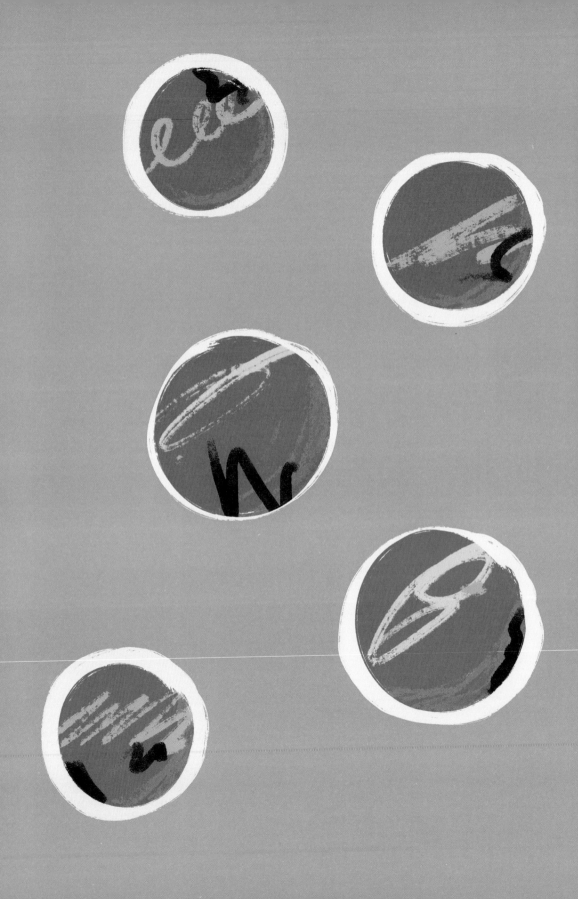

ROLL IT!

IT!

BLISS
OUT WITH
BALLS

EASY GRAB-AND-GO CAN SAVE THE DAY

We've all been there, those days where we're rushing out the door late for work, racing between meetings, or searching an airport desperately for something healthy to eat. Having something quick, easy and convenient to carry and enjoy on the go can be a snack game changer. That's where bliss balls and bites come in handy, especially those that can be stored at room temperature for longer periods of time. My tip is to choose one of my bliss-ball recipes in this chapter – or create your own using my 'build your own' guide on page 48 – make a big batch of them, and have them in the fridge or freezer, ready to take anywhere, anytime.

ROLL IT!

LUKE-SIZED LAMINGTONS

DF GF LC* PB SF

A delicious new take on my childhood favourite!

90 g (1 cup) desiccated or shredded
    coconut, for coating

CHOCOLATE Makes about 250 g (1 cup)
110 g (½ cup) cacao butter or coconut oil
60 g (½ cup) cacao powder
3 tablespoons maple syrup, coconut nectar,
    or maple-flavoured monk fruit syrup for
    low carb

FILLING
160 g (1 cup) raw macadamia nuts
155 g (1 cup) raw cashew nuts
90 g (1 cup) fine desiccated coconut
125 ml (½ cup) maple syrup, honey, coconut
    nectar, or maple-flavoured monk fruit
    syrup for low carb
3 tablespoons melted coconut oil, plus
    extra if needed
1 teaspoon vanilla bean paste or powder
125 g (1 cup) raspberries

Line two trays with baking paper.

For the filling, combine the nuts and coconut in a food processor and blitz to a fine meal. Pour in the sweetener, coconut oil and vanilla and blitz again until the mixture comes together to make a wet, sticky dough. If it's too dry, simply add a little extra coconut oil, 1 teaspoon at a time, to bring it to the right texture; if it's too wet, add more desiccated coconut.

Once you're happy with your dough, wrap 2–3 tablespoons of it around two raspberries, ensuring the raspberries stay together and none of their juice leaks out (this will be part of the explosion when you bite into each ball). Place the ball on one of the prepared trays. Repeat this process with the remaining dough and raspberries. You will end up with 16–18 medium to large balls – they are not designed to be bite-sized! Transfer the balls to the freezer to set.

For the chocolate, combine the cacao butter or coconut oil, cacao powder and sweetener in a saucepan over medium–low heat and melt, whisking, until smooth. Remove from the heat, cool slightly and try a small amount on the tip of your finger. For a darker chocolate, add more cacao powder; for a sweeter chocolate, add more sweetener, to suit your taste.

Set the chocolate aside for 10–15 minutes to cool and thicken, ready for coating your lamington balls.

Place the coconut in a shallow bowl. Using a fork or your fingers, dip each lamington ball in the cooled melted chocolate, then sprinkle with the coconut. You can completely cover or not. Transfer to the tray and return to the fridge or freezer for 10 minutes to set the chocolate. Serve at once or store in an airtight container in the fridge for up to 5 days or freeze for up to 1 month.

Makes 16–18

ROLL IT!

LEMON DELICIOUS

DF GF LC* PB SF

These balls are the ultimate bite-sized version of a lemon slice my nan used to make me. I'd go to her house and there it was: a nutty coconut base topped with a creamy lemony icing. I never could resist. Here's a really quick and simple way to re-create that flavour combination for the perfect snack any time of day.

240 g (1½ cups) raw macadamia nuts or cashew nuts

225 g (2½ cups) fine desiccated coconut, plus extra if needed

3 tablespoons maple syrup, honey, coconut nectar, or maple-flavoured monk fruit syrup for low carb

3 tablespoons coconut oil, plus extra if needed

1 teaspoon vanilla bean paste or powder

zest of 2 lemons, plus 2 tablespoons lemon juice

To get started, line a tray with baking paper.

Combine the macadamias or cashews and 180 g (2 cups) of the desiccated coconut in a food processor and blitz until a fine crumb forms.

Tip in the sweetener, coconut oil, vanilla and lemon zest and juice. Blitz again to make a thick, wet dough that can be rolled into balls easily. If it's too dry, add a little extra coconut oil; if it's too wet, add more desiccated coconut.

Place the remaining 45 g (½ cup) desiccated coconut in a shallow bowl. Use your hands to roll the dough into large walnut-sized balls, then coat each ball in the desiccated coconut. Place on the prepared tray and transfer to the fridge to firm up for 15 minutes. Enjoy at once or store in an airtight container in the fridge for up to 5 days or freeze for up to 1 month.

Makes about 20

SNACKABLE
FACT
Got some limes hanging around?
Don't let them go to waste. This
bliss-ball recipe actually works with
most types of citrus, so swap out
the lemons for limes, oranges or
blood oranges.

BLACK FOREST CAKE BOMBS

DF GF PB SF

Traditionally, a black forest cake is a combination of chocolate sponge, whipped cream and loads of cherries. My version celebrates the original in a way that gives you the same great taste without the need to bake a thing. Plus, you get all the incredible health benefits from using nutrient-dense ingredients.

155 g (1 cup) raw cashew nuts or
    macadamia nuts
180 g (2 cups) fine desiccated coconut,
    plus extra if needed
125 g blackberries
125 g pitted fresh cherries

3 tablespoons maple syrup, honey, coconut
    nectar or maple-flavoured monk
    fruit syrup
2 tablespoons coconut oil, plus extra
    if needed
250 g (1 cup) Chocolate (see page 40)

To get started, line a tray with baking paper.

Place the cashews or macadamias and desiccated coconut in a food processor or high-speed blender and pulse until well combined. Add the blackberries, cherries, sweetener and coconut oil and blitz again to make a thick, wet dough that can be rolled into balls easily. If it's too wet, add a little more desiccated coconut; if it's too dry, add more coconut oil.

Use your hands to roll the dough into large walnut-sized balls, then place on the prepared tray. Transfer the balls to the freezer to firm up for 15 minutes.

Meanwhile, prepare the chocolate and allow it to cool and thicken for 10–15 minutes, ready for coating your black forest balls.

Once the balls are cold, firm and set, use your fingers or a fork to dunk them into the chocolate. Place back on the tray and return to the fridge or freezer for 10 minutes to set the chocolate. Drizzle any leftover chocolate over the black forest balls to create fun patterns and return to the fridge until ready to serve. (If the leftover chocolate is too thick or firm, simply melt it over low heat to make it runny enough to work with again.) Store in an airtight container in the fridge for up to 5 days or freeze for up to 1 month.

Makes about 15

ROLL IT!

PEANUT BUTTER SNICKER SNACKS

DF GF PB SF

Four words for you: peanut butter snicker snacks. Now, try saying that three times quickly! A mouthful, right? Well, just wait till you try these – they are one of the yummiest soul-warming mouthfuls you ever will taste.

155 g (1 cup) raw cashew nuts or macadamia nuts
45 g (½ cup) fine desiccated coconut, plus extra if needed
135 g (½ cup) crunchy peanut butter, plus extra if needed
10 medjool dates, pitted and soaked in boiling water for 15 minutes, drained

3 tablespoons melted coconut oil, plus extra if needed
1 teaspoon vanilla bean paste or powder
250 g (1 cup) Chocolate (see page 40)
160 g (1 cup) roughly chopped toasted peanuts

Line a tray with baking paper.

Place the cashews or macadamias and desiccated coconut in a food processor and blitz until well combined. Add the peanut butter, dates, coconut oil and vanilla and blitz again to make a thick, wet dough that can be rolled into balls easily. If it's too wet, add a little extra desiccated coconut; if it's too dry, add more peanut butter or coconut oil.

Roll into extra-large walnut-sized balls and place on the prepared tray. Transfer to the fridge or freezer for 15 minutes to set and firm up.

Meanwhile, prepare the chocolate and allow it to cool and thicken for 10–15 minutes, ready for topping your peanut butter snicker balls.

Once the balls have set, remove from the fridge or freezer and, using a spoon, drizzle over the melted chocolate so it covers the top and runs down the sides. Then, working quickly before the chocolate sets, sprinkle over the chopped peanuts and return to the tray. Once you've done your entire batch, transfer to the fridge for 10–15 minutes to set completely. Store in an airtight container in the fridge for up to 5 days or freeze for up to 1 month.

Makes about 15

ROLL IT!

BUILD YOUR OWN
BLISS BALLS

Bliss balls are so versatile and can be made with such a delicious range of ingredients. Here is your ultimate bliss-ball guide that will allow you to create your favourite flavour combination.

Follow the outline below and for each component feel free to use one element straight up or try a combo of a few to make your perfect blend.

When experimenting with different ingredients, it's important to be intuitive. If your mixture is too dry, add some coconut oil or extra nut butter to loosen it up; if it's too wet, add some more desiccated coconut, almond meal, rolled oats or flaxseed meal to bring it all together.

Depending on the combination, your bliss balls can be DF, GF, LC, NF, PB or SF.

BASE
2 cups

almond meal
desiccated coconut
gluten-free rolled oats

NUT OR SEED BUTTER
2 cups

almond
cashew
coconut
hazelnut
macadamia
peanut
tahini

ROLL IT!

SEEDS
½ cup

chia
hemp
pumpkin
sesame
sunflower

SWEETENER
½ cup

coconut sugar
honey
maple syrup
monk fruit syrup
stevia

EXTRAS
to taste

cacao nibs
cacao powder
coconut oil
collagen powder
dried fruit
flaxseed meal
freeze-dried fruit
ground cinnamon
protein powder
roughly chopped nuts
vanilla bean paste or powder

METHOD

Place your preferred ingredients in a food processor or high-speed blender and blitz until well combined and a wet dough forms that is workable with your hands.

Roll the dough into 10 to 14 balls and transfer to the fridge or freezer to firm up for 15–20 minutes. Enjoy! Store in an airtight container in the fridge for up to 5 days or freeze for up to 1 month.

Makes 10–14

ROLL IT!

CHOCOLATE CHIP COOKIE DOUGH

DF GF LC* PB SF

Just the words 'cookie dough' bring to mind a ball of sticky goodness straight from the mixing bowl, so good you can hardly wait to bake it. This recipe will give you the equivalent mouth-watering reaction with the added benefit that it doesn't need to be baked.

200 g (2 cups) blanched almond meal or hazelnut meal, plus extra if needed
135 g (½ cup) smooth peanut, hazelnut or macadamia butter, plus extra if needed
3 tablespoons maple syrup, honey, coconut nectar, or maple-flavoured monk fruit syrup for low carb

3 tablespoons melted coconut oil, plus extra if needed
1 teaspoon vanilla bean paste or powder
250 g (1 cup) roughly chopped dark chocolate (80% cacao minimum or to make your own, see page 40)

Line a tray with baking paper.

Place the almond or hazelnut meal, nut butter, sweetener, coconut oil and vanilla in a food processor or high-speed blender and blitz to make a thick, wet dough that can be rolled into balls easily. If it's too dry, add more nut butter or coconut oil; if it's too wet, add more almond or hazelnut meal.

Once you're happy with the consistency, transfer the dough to a bowl and mix in the chocolate chunks. Use your hands to roll 2–3 tablespoons of dough per ball into evenly sized balls, then place on the prepared tray. I like the chocolate chunks to be showing and sticking out a little; it gives them a great look. Transfer the cookie dough balls to the fridge for 10–15 minutes to firm up. Store in an airtight container in the fridge for up to 5 days or freeze for up to 1 month.

Makes about 15

SNACKABLE FACT

If you don't have any dark chocolate on hand and can't be bothered making your own, you can use cacao nibs instead. Cacao nibs, tiny little pieces of crushed cacao beans, add a lovely crunch and bitterness to your balls.

SESAME AND HEMP BREKKIE BALLS

DF GF* NF PB SF

I wanted to create a bliss-ball recipe that would be suitable for kids to take to school, so making them nut free was important. At the same time, I wanted them to be packed with a great combo of ingredients that could be the ultimate breakfast on the go.

Please note: Although rolled oats labelled as gluten free contain negligible traces of gluten, they are not recommended for those who are allergic or those who have coeliac disease.

100 g (1 cup) gluten-free rolled oats
90 g (1 cup) fine desiccated coconut
3 tablespoons sunflower seeds
3 tablespoons hulled hemp seeds
2 tablespoons chia seeds
2 tablespoons sesame seeds

125 ml (½ cup) melted coconut oil
135 g (½ cup) hulled tahini
125 ml (½ cup) maple syrup, honey, coconut
     nectar or monk fruit syrup
1 teaspoon vanilla bean paste or powder
1 teaspoon ground cinnamon

Line a tray with baking paper.

Heat a frying pan over medium heat and add the rolled oats, desiccated coconut and sunflower seeds. Toss, keeping the mixture moving to prevent burning, for 3–4 minutes, or until the coconut is lightly browned and everything is aromatic.

Transfer the toasted mixture to a food processor and pulse three or four times, or until just slightly broken down. You don't want a fine crumb here, more small rough chunks. Tip into a large bowl, add the hemp seeds, chia seeds and sesame seeds and mix well with a spoon.

Add the coconut oil, tahini, sweetener, vanilla and cinnamon to the oat mixture. Mix with a large metal spoon to form a thick, wet dough that can be rolled into balls easily. If it's too dry, add more coconut oil or sweetener; if it's too wet, add more rolled oats or desiccated coconut.

Once you're happy with the consistency, use your hands to roll 2–3 tablespoons of dough per ball into evenly sized balls. Place them on the prepared tray and transfer to the fridge for 10–15 minutes to firm up. Store in an airtight container in the fridge for up to 1 week or freeze for up to 1 month.

Makes about 15

ROLL IT!

TURKISH DELIGHT BITES

DF GF LC* PB SF

Typically, Turkish delight is a jelly-like sweet treat made up predominantly of sugar flavoured with rosewater. Super fancy versions can include dates, walnuts and even chocolate. This recipe is my modern take on the classic flavour – and I've added some elements that will keep you feeling fuller for longer.

280 g (2 cups) raw pistachio nuts
100 g (1 cup) raw walnuts
90 g (1 cup) fine desiccated coconut
250 g (1 cup) cashew butter
3 tablespoons melted coconut oil
3 tablespoons maple syrup, honey, coconut
    nectar, or maple-flavoured monk fruit
    syrup for low carb

1–2 tablespoons rosewater, to taste
250 g (1 cup) Chocolate (see page 40)
20 g (½ cup) small edible dried rose
    petals (optional)

Line a tray with baking paper.

Heat a frying pan over medium heat and add half the pistachios, the walnuts and desiccated coconut. Toss, keeping the nuts moving to prevent burning, for 3–4 minutes, or until the coconut is lightly browned and everything is aromatic.

Transfer the toasted mixture to a food processor and blitz to a fine crumb. Add the cashew butter, coconut oil, sweetener and rosewater and blitz again to make a thick, wet dough that can be rolled into balls easily. If it's too dry, add a little more coconut oil or cashew butter; if it's too wet, add a little more desiccated coconut.

Once you're happy with the consistency, use your hands to roll 2–3 tablespoons of dough per ball into evenly sized balls. Spread them out on the prepared tray and transfer to the fridge for 10–15 minutes to firm up.

Meanwhile, prepare the chocolate and allow it to cool and thicken for 10–15 minutes, ready for coating your Turkish delight bites. This is a good time to lightly toast and roughly chop the remaining pistachios.

Once the balls are cold, firm and set, use your fingers or a fork to dunk them into the melted chocolate. Then, working quickly before the chocolate sets, sprinkle over the roughly chopped toasted pistachios and rose petals (if using) and return to the tray. Return to the fridge or freezer for 10–15 minutes to set the chocolate. Store in an airtight container in the fridge for up to 1 week or freeze for up to 1 month.

Makes about 15

ROLL IT!

WORK IT!

FUEL YOUR GOALS

Learning how to snack smart has been a real game changer for me in terms of sticking to and reaching my fitness goals. My mental and physical performance has increased tenfold and all it took was a few small tweaks in my snack game to get my training game on point. From a pre-workout perspective, too often I went into a session either underfed or overfed. I'd either not had any type of snack, meaning I was running on empty, or I'd had a meal that was way too big, and instead of training well, my body was focused on digesting rather than moving. Enjoying a bite-sized snack or drink designed to have before training will elevate your workout, and you'll get the most from your time spent exercising. But don't let all your hard work go to waste – refuelling and recovering after exercise is just as important as how you fuel yourself in the first place. You need all the goodness from real food to repair and nourish your body after you've worked hard. Remember: it's not what we do in the session, but how we repair and rebuild afterwards that changes us for the better. And don't go thinking just because you worked out, you can indulge in a naughty snack; you can't out-train a bad diet.

BEET YOUR BEST

DF GF LC* NF PB SF

A lot of store-bought pre-workout drinks can contain more numbers, colours and flavours than actual real food ingredients. This pre-workout beetroot drink ticks all the boxes when it comes to what you need for sustained energy, vascular pump and electrolytes.

1 beetroot, peeled and diced
250 g (1 cup) frozen raspberries
250 ml (1 cup) coconut water
1 tablespoon hemp seeds

1 lime, peeled and diced
1 tablespoon honey, maple syrup, coconut nectar, or maple-flavoured monk fruit syrup for low carb

Place all the ingredients in a food processor or high-speed blender and blitz until everything is smooth and well combined. Pour into a tall glass and enjoy 30 minutes before exercise.

Serves 1

SNACKABLE FACT

Beetroot is nature's original pre-workout hero, with research showing it not only boosts performance and endurance, but improves blood and oxygen flow, making it great for both cardio and strength.

PRE-WORKOUT CHOC–CAYENNE COFFEE

DF GF LC NF PB SF

When I head over to Los Angeles there's a health-food cafe I go to the moment I touch down to refresh and recharge after the long flight. It's called Kreation, and it lives up to its name with the most incredible smoothie, shot and elixir creations. My go-to is their 'loaded gun latte' that's packed with everything to supercharge your day or workout. Here is my version, with a few tweaks and additions to give your next workout a massive kick in the butt.

1–2 shots espresso coffee
3 tablespoons canned coconut cream
1 tablespoon MCT oil (optional)
½ teaspoon cacao powder
½ teaspoon vanilla bean paste or powder

¼ teaspoon ground cinnamon
pinch of cayenne pepper
70 g (½ cup) ice cubes, to serve (optional)
1 teaspoon roasted coffee beans, crushed

Place the coffee, coconut cream, MCT oil, cacao powder, vanilla, cinnamon and cayenne pepper in a high-speed blender and blitz on high until everything is smooth, well combined and the MCT oil has emulsified.

Place the ice cubes (if using) in a tall glass, pour over the coffee, then sprinkle on the crushed coffee beans. Enjoy 30 minutes before exercise.

Serves 1

SNACKABLE FACT

MCT stands for medium-chain triglycerides, a form of healthy fatty acids derived from coconut oil. They can improve energy, satiation and mental focus, making them a great addition to this pre-workout combo. When it comes to introducing MCT oil into your diet, always start small – with 1 teaspoon – and work your way up, as it can unsettle your tummy if you go too hard too fast.

RASPBERRY GRANOLA BARS

DF GF* LC* NF* PB SF

One of my favourite pre-workout snacks, this simple bar to enjoy anywhere, anytime has all the energy and nutrients of a big bowl of muesli with fruit and yoghurt. The rolled oats provide a sustained source of energy, with carbs from the fruit and sweetener, and satiating fats from the nuts and coconut.

350 g (3½ cups) gluten-free rolled oats
30 g (½ cup) shredded coconut
160 g (1 cup) macadamia nuts (or sunflower seeds for nut free), roughly chopped
50 g (½ cup) flaxseed meal
90 g (½ cup) coconut sugar
250 ml (1 cup) maple syrup, honey, coconut nectar, or maple-flavoured monk fruit syrup for low carb

1 teaspoon vanilla bean paste or powder
125 ml (½ cup) room temperature coconut oil

RASPBERRY FILLING
375 g (3 cups) fresh or frozen and thawed raspberries
1 tablespoon white chia seeds
1 tablespoon arrowroot or tapioca flour

Preheat the oven to 180°C and line a 20 cm square cake tin with baking paper.

To make the raspberry filling, place the raspberries and chia seeds in a small saucepan over medium–low heat and cook, stirring and mashing up the raspberries with a wooden spoon or spatula, for 3–4 minutes, or until starting to bubble and turn jam-like. Stir in the arrowroot or tapioca flour to thicken, then remove from the heat and set aside to cool slightly.

Meanwhile, combine 200 g (2 cups) of oats, half the shredded coconut and macadamias or sunflower seeds in a food processor and blitz to make a fine crumb-like flour. Tip into a bowl, add the remaining oats, coconut, macadamias or sunflower seeds, flaxseed meal and coconut sugar and mix well.

Pour in the sweetener, vanilla and coconut oil and, using a spoon or spatula, mix well to form a moist, crumbly granola mixture.

Place half the granola mixture in the prepared tin, pressing it firmly and evenly into the base and up the sides with your hands. Top with an even layer of the raspberry filling, then scatter over the remaining granola mixture, keeping it rough and rustic; you want it to resemble the top of an apple crumble. Bake for 20–30 minutes, or until golden brown and crunchy looking on top. Set aside to cool for 10 minutes, then transfer to the fridge to cool completely.

Remove the granola slice from the tin and cut into 12 bars or portions of your liking. Store in an airtight containerin the fridge for up to 5 days or freeze for up to 3 months.

Makes 12

NO-BAKE CHOC-CHARGER COLLAGEN BARS

DF GF SF

If you're looking for pre-workout energy or post-workout recovery with the perfect performance-enhancing combination of healthy fats, carbs and protein, then look no further. Using natural collagen powder, which can be found in health-food stores and some supermarkets, adds a flavour-free boost that can support muscle repair and growth, along with healthy hair, skin and nails.

180 g (1 cup) pitted medjool dates
270 g (1 cup) cashew nut, macadamia nut or peanut butter
3 tablespoons maple syrup, honey, coconut nectar or monk fruit syrup

50 g (½ cup) unflavoured collagen powder
60 g (½ cup) cacao powder
2 teaspoons maca powder
1 teaspoon vanilla bean paste or powder
3 tablespoons cacao nibs

Place the dates in a food processor and blitz until broken up and mushy. Add the nut butter and sweetener and blitz again to combine and make a wet paste. Add the collagen, cacao powder, maca powder and vanilla and blitz until everything comes together to form a thick dough.

Place the dough on a piece of baking paper. Roll into a ball, then roll out into a log about 30 cm long. Use your hands to press the log down flat, creating a long, flat rectangle about 35 cm × 10 cm in size.

Scatter the cacao nibs over the top and press them in gently with your hands. Use a knife to cut into evenly sized bars. Store in an airtight container in the fridge for up to 1 week or freeze for up to 1 month.

Makes 10

SNACKABLE FACT

Hailing from Peru, maca is a really powerful plant. The root is turned into a powder that is often referred to as an adaptogen. This adaptogen plays a role in supporting our hormones and increasing our libido, energy and endurance.

PROTEIN-PACKED SMOOTHIE BOWL

Smoothie bowls are one of my ultimate go-to pre- or post-workout snacks, as they're loaded with a great balance of carbs, healthy fats and protein. Here is your ultimate smoothie-bowl guide that will allow you to create your favourite flavour combination.

Follow the outline below and for each component feel free to use one element straight up or try a combo of a few to make your perfect blend.

When experimenting with different ingredients, it's important to be intuitive. If your smoothie bowl is too thick, add some more liquid of choice to get it moving; if it's too runny, add more frozen fruit to thicken it up.

Depending on what combo you create, your smoothie bowls can be DF, GF, LC, NF, PB or SF.

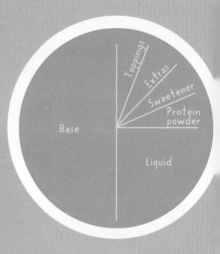

BASE	LIQUID
2 cups (frozen)	250 ml (1 cup)
blackberries	almond milk
blueberries	apple juice
chopped banana	coconut milk
chopped pineapple	coconut water
diced mango	filtered water
pure acai	hemp seed milk
raspberries	macadamia nut milk
strawberries	

PROTEIN POWDER

to taste

collagen powder
plant-based protein
whey

EXTRAS

to taste

avocado
cacao powder
ground cinnamon
ice cubes
spirulina
vanilla bean paste or powder

SWEETENER

to taste (optional)

coconut sugar
honey
maple syrup
monk fruit syrup
stevia

TOPPINGS

to taste

bee pollen
cacao nibs
fresh fruit
muesli or granola
nut butter
shredded coconut

METHOD

Place your preferred ingredients in a food processor or high-speed blender and blitz until well combined. Pour into a deep bowl and finish with your favourite combination of toppings.

Serves 1

LEMON–LIME SPLICE PROTEIN BARS

DF GF LC* NF SF

This is a fantastic recipe for those looking for a zesty and light protein bar that can also be adapted to be low carb and keto friendly. To make it low carb, simply use your preferred monk fruit syrup instead of maple, honey or coconut nectar; it's that simple.

375 g (1½ cups) coconut butter
125 ml (½ cup) coconut oil
125 ml (½ cup) maple syrup, honey, coconut nectar, or monk fruit syrup for low carb
100 g (1 cup) unflavoured collagen powder

finely grated zest and juice of 1 lemon
finely grated zest and juice of 1 lime
1 teaspoon vanilla bean paste or powder
30 g (½ cup) shredded coconut

Line a 20 cm square cake tin with baking paper.

Place the coconut butter, coconut oil, sweetener, collagen powder, lemon and lime juice and vanilla in a food processor or high-speed blender and blitz until smooth and thick. Add the shredded coconut and pulse a few times to incorporate without breaking it up too much.

Pour the protein bar mixture into the prepared tin, scatter over the lemon and lime zest and transfer to the freezer for 45 minutes to set completely.

Slice into 10 bars and enjoy. Store in an airtight container in the fridge for up to 1 week or freeze for up to 1 month.

Makes 10

SNACKABLE FACT

Coconut butter is made using 100 per cent coconut flesh and is the same consistency as other nut butters, such as peanut, almond or macadamia. It can be found in most health-food stores and online. Sometimes the firmer flesh settles to the bottom of the jar and the looser oil sits at the top, so make sure you get in there with a spoon and give it a good mix before using.

PEANUT BUTTER POST-WORKOUT PARFAIT

DF GF* NF* SF

What if I told you I've created the ultimate post-workout snack that is almost better than dessert? Well, ladies and gentlemen, this is it! One of the things I love most about this parfait is you can easily make a massive batch of the granola so you always have some on hand for this recipe and when you're on the go; multiply the quantities accordingly.

250 g (1 cup) vanilla bean or plain coconut yoghurt
155 g (1 cup) fresh or frozen blueberries

PEANUT BUTTER GRANOLA
3 tablespoons smooth peanut butter, plus extra 3 tablespoons to drizzle
3 tablespoons maple syrup, honey, coconut nectar or monk fruit syrup

2 tablespoons melted coconut oil
100 g (1 cup) gluten-free rolled oats (see page 16)
80 g (½ cup) roughly chopped raw macadamia nuts
3 tablespoons unflavoured collagen powder
1 teaspoon vanilla bean paste or powder
3 tablespoons shredded coconut

Preheat the oven to 160°C and line a large baking tray with baking paper.

To make the peanut butter granola, place the peanut butter, sweetener and coconut oil in a bowl and mix to combine. In a separate bowl, combine the rolled oats, macadamia nuts, collagen powder and vanilla and mix well. Pour the wet ingredients into the dry ingredients and mix until all the dry ingredients are incorporated. Tip onto the prepared tray and spread out, making sure it's nice and flat so it cooks evenly. Bake for 8–10 minutes. Carefully remove the tray from the oven, add the shredded coconut and give everything a good mix. Return to the oven and bake for a further 6–8 minutes, or until the shredded coconut is lightly golden brown. Set aside to cool completely. This is when the granola becomes nice and crispy.

Break the granola into small clusters and begin to layer up your parfaits. Using a wide, tall glass, start with a few tablespoons of granola, followed by 1–2 tablespoons of yoghurt and a small handful of blueberries, then repeat all the way to the top, finishing with a blueberry layer and a drizzle of extra peanut butter. Repeat this process until you have four parfaits in total. Dig in.

Serves 4

MUSCLE MONKEY MUFFINS

DF GF LC NF* SF

If you're looking to pack on some extra lean muscle mass while keeping your tastebuds happy, these cheeky little muffins have got you covered. If you want to mix up the flavours a little, feel free to use a flavoured collagen powder: chocolate or strawberry varieties work amazingly well.

4 eggs
2 large very ripe bananas, mashed
125 ml (½ cup) maple syrup, honey,
    coconut nectar or maple-flavoured
    monk fruit syrup
135 g (½ cup) peanut, macadamia nut
    or almond butter

200 g (2 cups) blanched almond meal
50 g (½ cup) unflavoured collagen powder
1 teaspoon gluten-free baking powder
1 teaspoon vanilla bean paste or powder
¼ teaspoon sea salt

Preheat the oven to 160°C and line a 12-hole muffin tin with paper cases.

Crack the eggs into a large bowl and whisk until frothy. Add the mashed banana, sweetener and nut butter and mix with a wooden spoon or spatula to form a thick, wet batter. Add the almond meal, collagen powder, baking powder, vanilla and salt and stir until well combined.

Spoon the batter evenly into the prepared muffin tin and bake for 15–20 minutes, or until golden brown on top and a skewer inserted in the centre of a muffin comes out clean. Best enjoyed straight away. Store in an airtight container in the fridge for up to 1 week or freeze for up to 1 month.

Makes 12

SNACKABLE FACT

These muffins can be made nut free by swapping the 200 g (2 cups) of almond meal for 125 g (1 cup) of arrowroot or tapioca flour and 130 g (1 cup) of coconut flour, and switching the nut butter for tahini.

ROASTED MACADAMIA PROTEIN COOKIES

DF GF SF

I love baking and eating all sorts of cookies, but my default when I make them is always chocolate chip. I thought it was about time I mixed things up and created something a little different though equally as amazing. I can't wait for you to try these.

270 g (1 cup) macadamia nut butter, plus extra if needed
2 eggs, whisked
3 tablespoons melted coconut oil, plus extra if needed
90 g (½ cup) coconut sugar
50 g (½ cup) unflavoured collagen powder, plus extra if needed

2 tablespoons coconut flour
1 teaspoon vanilla bean paste or powder
1 teaspoon gluten-free baking powder
¼ teaspoon sea salt
80 g (½ cup) raw macadamia nuts, lightly toasted and roughly chopped

Preheat the oven to 180°C and line a large baking tray with baking paper.

Place the macadamia nut butter, eggs and coconut oil in a large bowl and mix with a wooden spoon or spatula until well combined. Add the coconut sugar, collagen powder, coconut flour, vanilla, baking powder and salt and mix to form a slightly sticky, workable dough. If it's too dry and crumbly, add a little more nut butter or coconut oil; if it's too wet, add a little more collagen powder.

Fold the toasted macadamias into the dough, then dollop tablespoon amounts onto the prepared tray, allowing a 5 cm space between each. Use the back of your spoon to press down slightly on each cookie to create a flat top. Bake for 6–8 minutes, or until the cookies are just golden brown around the edges and still a little gooey in the middle. Allow to cool slightly before transferring to a wire rack to cool completely. Store in an airtight container in the pantry for up to 3 days, in the fridge for up to 1 week or freeze for up to 1 month.

Makes 12–14

ARNIE BANARNIE BOWL

GF NF SF

Yes, that's right, this is inspired by Arnie, the kindergarten cop himself. You'll 'be back' and heading straight 'for the chopper' once you've devoured this post-workout energy bowl, with its epic dose of quality protein and smart carbs.

200 g (1 cup) sliced frozen banana
150 g (1 cup) diced frozen mango
125 ml (½ cup) coconut water, plus extra
    if needed
2 tablespoons unflavoured collagen powder

TOPPING
80 g (½ cup) fresh or frozen blueberries
1 small banana, sliced into discs
1 passionfruit, pulp and seeds
1 teaspoon cacao nibs

Place the frozen banana and mango, coconut water and collagen powder in a food processor or high-speed blender and pulse until thick, smooth and creamy. Pour into a bowl.

Top your energy bowl with the blueberries, sliced banana, passionfruit pulp and seeds, and cacao nibs. Hasta la vista, baby!

Serves 1

SNACKABLE FACT

I've deliberately left out some of the healthy fats I quite often use, such as coconut cream, peanut butter and nuts, as they can slow down the way we metabolise our carbs and protein, and post-workout, we want that immediate hit of recovery fuel to go straight to our muscles, no messing around.

WORK IT!

DIP
IT!

DIG INTO
THESE
CRACKERS,
CHIPS 'N' DIPS

IT STARTS WITH REAL FOOD

I've always been a big believer in cooking from scratch with real food. It's only once we're hands-on with what we're making that we can truly understand and control what goes into what we're eating. You'd be horrified by the contents of many store-bought snacks that are advertised as clean, healthy and good for you. There is a term called 'greenwashing' that describes a trick many food and supplement companies use to make something sound and look far better for you than it is. Brown, earthy packaging or branding colours and the use of the words 'real', 'natural' or 'farm fresh' help create an impression that the processed food is healthy when, in fact, a quick look at the label will have you scratching your head wondering what farm produces ingredients that have numbers for names. The way around it? Cook from scratch and know where your ingredients come from. Knowing where your food was grown, caught, raised and produced and how it was transported enables you to make better choices for the sake of your own health and that of the planet. Health starts in the kitchen; it provides you with the best tools for ultimate wellbeing, happiness and longevity.

ZUCCHINI DIPPERS WITH AVO SALSA

DF GF LC SF

SNACKABLE FACT

Removing excess liquid from the zucchini helps your crackers become extra crispy. The best way to do this is to spread the grated zucchini out on a clean tea towel and roll up the tea towel to enclose, then hold it over the sink and give it all a good twist and squeeze. You'll be amazed at how much liquid you extract.

I created this recipe so you could enjoy a crispy cracker and get a decent daily dose of nourishing greens without even noticing. The zucchini acts as a fantastic base for these crackers that I like to call dippers, as they're great for dipping into your favourite dips – or topping with this zesty salsa.

Please note: Flax or chia eggs aren't a suitable substitute for eggs in this recipe.

DIPPERS
270 g (2 cups) grated zucchini, squeezed
   of excess liquid
8 eggs
65 g (½ cup) coconut flour
50 g (½ cup) blanched almond meal
60 g (½ cup) tapioca flour
125 ml (½ cup) melted coconut oil
2 tablespoons nutritional yeast flakes
2 teaspoons garlic powder
2 teaspoons onion powder
2 teaspoons gluten-free baking powder

AVO SALSA
2 avocados, finely diced
200 g yellow cherry tomatoes, finely diced
zest and juice of 1 lime, plus extra lime
   juice to serve
1 tablespoon extra-virgin olive oil
1 teaspoon chilli flakes
1 tablespoon finely chopped flat-leaf
   parsley leaves
sea salt and freshly ground black pepper

Preheat the oven to 180°C and line two baking trays with baking paper.

Place all the dippers ingredients in a food processor and pulse to form a smooth and workable dough.

Evenly divide the dipper dough between the prepared trays, spread out to the edges and flatten until about 5 mm thick. You can place a piece of baking paper on top and use a rolling pin to make it perfectly flat if you like, otherwise just press with your hands. Bake for 15 minutes, or until just turning lightly golden. Remove from the oven and carefully flip the par-baked dipper dough over on each tray, then slice into 6 cm × 6 cm squares. Return the trays to the oven and bake for 15 minutes, or until the dippers are golden brown on top. The longer you cook them, the crispier they become, so keep an eye on them to get your desired consistency. Set aside to cool slightly.

For the avo salsa, place the avocado, tomato, lime zest and juice and olive oil in a bowl. Toss well to combine. Sprinkle over the chilli flakes and parsley, season with salt and pepper and squeeze over the extra lime juice to taste.

Enjoy the zucchini dippers topped with the avo salsa. Store the zucchini dippers in an airtight container in the fridge for up to 5 days or freeze for up to 1 month.

Serves 8–12

GARLIC PITA BREAD WITH LEMONY TAHINI DIP

DF GF SF

Tahini is wonderfully versatile – it makes the perfect nut-free substitute for ingredients like peanut or almond butter, plus it suits both sweet and savoury dishes. When incorporated with fresh herbs, as I've done here, it's a winning combo.

Please note: Flax or chia eggs aren't a suitable substitute for eggs in this recipe.

2 tablespoons butter, olive oil or
    coconut butter

LEMONY TAHINI DIP
30 g (1 cup) torn coriander leaves
20 g (1 cup) torn flat-leaf parsley leaves
125 ml (½ cup) extra-virgin olive oil
135 g (½ cup) hulled tahini
125 ml (½ cup) freshly squeezed
    lemon juice
3 garlic cloves, finely chopped
1 teaspoon sea salt

PITA BREAD
260 g (2 cups) arrowroot or tapioca flour,
    plus extra if needed
50 g (½ cup) blanched almond meal
2 eggs
250 ml (1 cup) canned coconut milk,
    plus extra if needed
1 teaspoon sea salt
½ teaspoon garlic powder
½ teaspoon onion powder

To make the lemony tahini dip, place the herbs in a food processor and pulse three or four times to chop into smaller pieces. Add the olive oil, tahini, lemon juice, garlic and salt and blitz until well combined, smooth and creamy. Cover and set aside in the fridge.

To get started on the pita bread, combine the arrowroot or tapioca flour, almond meal, eggs, coconut milk, salt and garlic and onion powders and whisk well to form a smooth, thick but slightly runny batter. If your batter is too thick, add more coconut milk; if it's too thin, add a dash more arrowroot or tapioca flour.

Melt your preferred cooking fat in a large frying pan over medium–high heat. Using a 125 ml (½ cup) measuring cup, measure out the batter, pour into the hot pan and cook, flipping halfway through, for 5–6 minutes, or until the pita is lightly golden brown on each side. Transfer to a plate lined with paper towel. Repeat with the remaining batter to get six pita breads.

Spoon the dip into a small serving bowl, place the still-warm pita breads on a platter and serve. Store leftover pita breads in an airtight container in the fridge for up to 5 days or freeze for up to 1 month.

Serves 4–6

SNACKABLE FACT

Tahini has a great nutritional profile in that it's high in anti-inflammatory healthy fats, low in carbs and packed with vitamin B6. B vitamins are a really important component of our diet, as they help the body produce energy.

SEED CRACKERS

Seed crackers are one of the simplest snacks you can make in bulk to have on hand when you need something quick and easy. Here is the ultimate seed-cracker guide that will allow you to create your favourite flavour combination. Enjoy straight up or pair with your preferred dip.

Follow the outline below and for the mixed seed component it's important to use a variety for contrast, texture and flavour. Feel free to use any combo of herbs and spices to create your perfect crackers.

When experimenting with different ingredients it's important to be intuitive. If your seed mixture is too dry, add a little more water; if it's too wet, add more dry ingredients of choice to thicken.

Depending on what combo you create, your crackers can be DF, GF, LC, NF, PB or SF.

Mixed
seeds

Liquid
base

Herbs &
spices | Binder

MIXED SEEDS
(MIX AND MATCH)
2½ cups

flaxseeds
hemp seeds
pumpkin seeds
sesame seeds
sunflower seeds

BINDER
2 tablespoons

ground chia seeds
ground flaxseeds
psyllium husks

LIQUID BASE
500 ml (2 cups)

filtered water
maple syrup or honey
(for sweet crackers)

HERBS AND SPICES
2 teaspoons

chilli flakes/powder
curry powder
dried basil
dried oregano
dried thyme
garlic powder
ground turmeric
Italian seasoning
Mexican seasoning
nori
nutritional yeast
onion powder
paprika
seaweed
za'atar

METHOD

Preheat the oven to 150°C and line two baking trays with baking paper.

Place the mixed seeds, binder and herbs and spices in a large bowl and mix well with a spoon. Pour in the liquid base and stir to combine. Set aside for 20–30 minutes to thicken to a gel-like consistency.

Once nice and sticky, pour the cracker dough evenly over the prepared trays and spread out with a spatula until 5 mm thick. Bake, keeping a close eye on them so the crackers don't burn, for 50–60 minutes, or until lightly golden brown and crispy.

Remove from the oven and allow to cool completely before cutting, cracking or eating. Store the seed crackers in an airtight container in the pantry for up to 2 weeks.

Serves 8–10

TIP

To get perfectly shaped seed crackers each and every time, score the cracker dough with a knife halfway through baking. Alternatively, for something more rustic, use your hands to crack them into shapes before serving.

DIPS AHOY

DF GF LC PB SF

FOUR DIPS
AND MIXED VEG

You'll die for these dips once you taste them!
Too often we fall into the habit or convenience
of buying store-bought dips, yet it's so easy to
make your own. A lot of the commercial varieties
contain unnecessary oils, sweeteners and
fillers that compromise taste and health. Make
these four part of your staples at home and pair
with any number of my toppers, crackers
or flatbreads or simply add freshly cut veg.

1. INCREDIBLE CAPSICUM
AND CASHEW DIP

2. SWEET POTATO AND
MACADAMIA DIP

3. CHILLI AND ROAST
PUMPKIN DIP

4. PISTACHIO PESTO DIP

INCREDIBLE CAPSICUM AND CASHEW DIP

3 red capsicums, cored and quartered
125 ml (½ cup) extra-virgin olive oil, plus
    extra 1–2 tablespoons to drizzle
1 long red chilli, roughly chopped
3 garlic cloves, roughly chopped
310 g (2 cups) raw cashew nuts, soaked in
    boiling water for 15 minutes, drained

125 ml (½ cup) canned coconut cream
3 tablespoons freshly squeezed lemon juice
sea salt and freshly ground black pepper
1 teaspoon chilli flakes
3 tablespoons finely chopped flat-leaf
    parsley leaves (optional)

Preheat the oven to 200°C and line a baking tray with baking paper.

Place the capsicum on the prepared tray, drizzle over 1–2 tablespoons of the oil and roast for 20 minutes. Add the chilli and garlic, gently toss and roast for another 10 minutes, or until the capsicum is blackened and blistered and the garlic and chilli are softened and aromatic.

Transfer the capsicum to a heatproof bowl, cover with plastic wrap (this helps it sweat, making the skin easier to remove) and set aside for 5–10 minutes, or until cool enough to handle. Carefully peel away and discard the blistered skin from the capsicum, then transfer the soft flesh to a food processor with the roasted chilli and garlic.

Add the cashew nuts, the remaining 125 ml (½ cup) of oil, the coconut cream and lemon juice to the food processor, season well with salt and pepper and blitz to form a smooth yet slightly chunky dip. If your dip is too dry, add a little extra oil. Once you're happy with the consistency, spoon into a serving bowl, sprinkle over the chilli flakes and parsley (if using) and you're good to go.

Makes about 3 cups

SWEET POTATO AND MACADAMIA DIP

2–3 small sweet potatoes (about 400 g), scrubbed
125 ml (½ cup) extra-virgin olive oil, plus extra if needed
½ red onion, finely diced
2 garlic cloves, finely diced
1 long red chilli, finely diced
125 ml (½ cup) freshly squeezed lemon juice

1 tablespoon apple cider vinegar
240 g (1½ cups) raw macadamia nuts, soaked in boiling water for 15 minutes, drained, plus extra if needed
2 teaspoons curry powder
1 teaspoon smoked paprika
sea salt and freshly ground black pepper

Preheat the oven to 200°C and line a baking tray with baking paper.

Pierce each sweet potato all over with a fork, place on the prepared tray and drizzle with 2 tablespoons of the olive oil. Roast for 30–45 minutes, or until softened and completely cooked through. (The reason I recommend using small sweet potatoes, rather than large, is to cut down on cooking time.) Set aside until cool enough to handle. Peel off and discard the skin and transfer all the flesh to a food processor.

Meanwhile, heat 2 tablespoons of the remaining oil in a large frying pan over medium–high heat, add the onion, garlic and chilli and saute for 3–4 minutes, or until the onion is translucent and the garlic is lightly golden brown and aromatic. Add to the sweet potato in the food processor.

Add the remaining oil, the lemon juice, vinegar, macadamia nuts, curry powder and paprika to the food processor and season generously with salt and pepper. Blitz until everything comes together to form a thick, smooth and creamy dip. If it's looking a little dry, add some more oil; if it's a little wet, add some more macadamia nuts. Spoon into a serving bowl and enjoy.

Makes about 3 cups

CHILLI AND ROAST PUMPKIN DIP

1 kg butternut pumpkin, peeled and cut
   into 2.5 cm cubes
165 ml extra-virgin olive oil, plus extra
   if needed
sea salt and freshly ground black pepper

125 ml (½ cup) freshly squeezed lemon juice
2 teaspoons chilli flakes, plus extra to serve
1 teaspoon ground cumin
1 teaspoon ground coriander
1 teaspoon smoked paprika

Preheat the oven to 200°C and line a large baking tray with baking paper.

Place the pumpkin on the prepared tray, drizzle over 2 tablespoons of the oil and season well with salt and pepper. Roast for 30–45 minutes, or until lightly golden, softened and completely cooked through. Transfer to a large food processor.

Add the remaining oil, the lemon juice and spices to the food processor and season generously with salt. Blitz until well combined, smooth and creamy. If your dip is too dry, add a little extra oil until you've reached your desired consistency. Spoon the dip into a serving bowl, sprinkle over some extra chilli flakes or smoked paprika and dig in.

Makes about 4 cups

PISTACHIO PESTO DIP

30 g (2 loosely packed cups) basil leaves
20 g (2 loosely packed cups) flat-leaf
   parsley leaves
140 g (1 cup) raw pistachio nuts
3 garlic cloves, crushed

zest and juice of 2 lemons
125 ml (½ cup) extra-virgin olive oil,
   or to taste
sea salt and freshly ground black pepper

Place the herbs, pistachio nuts, garlic and lemon zest and juice in a food processor and blitz until roughly combined and the herbs have broken down a little.

With the motor running, slowly drizzle in the olive oil and process until the dip reaches your desired consistency. For a chunkier dip, use less oil and more nuts; for a smoother dip, use more oil and blitz for longer. Season to taste with salt and pepper, spoon into a serving bowl and eat.

Makes about 2 cups

DIP IT!

MY FAMOUS SWEET POTATO FRIES WITH CHILLI–LIME AIOLI

DF GF LC NF PB* SF

SNACKABLE FACT

If you can't be bothered making your own chilli-lime aioli or you'd like to make this recipe vegan friendly, simply purchase a store-bought variety. Just be sure to read the label and avoid highly refined seed oils – olive oil is best – and make sure there are no hidden sugars or fillers that should never be in aioli.

So, these sweet potato fries have become a bit of a phenomenon lately because I have finally figured out how to get crispy fries each and every time. No longer will you be subjected to limp or soggy, these failproof fries are the real deal. Pair them with a vegan aioli to make the whole meal plant based.

SWEET POTATO FRIES
2 sweet potatoes (about 500 g), peeled
3 tablespoons extra-virgin olive oil
60 g (½ cup) arrowroot or tapioca flour
1 teaspoon smoked paprika
½ teaspoon garlic powder
½ teaspoon onion powder
sea salt

CHILLI–LIME AIOLI Makes 250 g (1 cup)
4 egg yolks
2 teaspoons dijon mustard
2 tablespoons apple cider vinegar
juice of 1–2 limes
3 garlic cloves, peeled
1 teaspoon cayenne pepper, or to taste
sea salt and freshly ground black pepper
400 ml extra-virgin olive oil

Preheat the oven to 200°C and line two baking trays with baking paper.

Slice your sweet potato into 7 cm long × 5 mm wide fries. Making sure they are all about the same size is important here for even cooking and uniform crispiness.

Place the fries in a large bowl, drizzle over the olive oil and toss with your hands to coat well. Add the arrowroot or tapioca flour, paprika, garlic and onion powders and 2 teaspoons of salt and, again, toss with your hands to get all-over even coverage and distribution of flavour.

Carefully spread out the fries in a single layer on the prepared trays, making sure there is no overlap (this helps them get extra crispy). Roast for 20–30 minutes, or until they are golden brown, crunchy and crispy. (Roasting times can vary based on your oven and how thinly you cut the fries, so keep an eye on them, as – much like Melbourne's weather – they can turn very quickly.)

Meanwhile, for the chilli–lime aioli, place the egg yolks, mustard, vinegar, juice of one lime, garlic, cayenne pepper and a pinch of salt in a large bowl. Whiz together using a hand-held blender. With the hand-held blender still going, slowly pour in the olive oil in a thin, even stream until all the oil has been incorporated and the aioli is thick and creamy – take your time so it doesn't split. Add extra lime juice to thin, if needed. Alternatively, you can use a food processor. Season well with salt and pepper to taste and check you're happy with the level of heat. Spoon into a serving bowl, cover with plastic wrap and refrigerate until needed.

Transfer the fries to a large tray or platter, season well with salt and pepper and pair with the chilli–lime aioli.

Serves 2

'CHICKEN' SALT
POTATO CRISPS

DF GF NF PB SF

Crisps are one of my favourite guilty pleasures in life, and I am not sure if knowing how to make my own is a blessing or a curse. But what I do know is that they are quick, simple and delicious – and by far beat any store-bought variation. If you'd like to have some chicken salt on hand down the track, feel free to scale up the recipe. Store it in an airtight container in the pantry.

1 kg potatoes, scrubbed
3 tablespoons extra-virgin olive oil
sea salt

'CHICKEN' SALT
1 teaspoon fine sea salt
½ teaspoon sweet paprika
¼ teaspoon coconut sugar
¼ teaspoon garlic powder
¼ teaspoon onion powder

Preheat the oven to 200°C and line two baking trays with baking paper.

Combine the chicken salt ingredients in a small bowl and mix well. Set aside.

Using a mandoline or very sharp knife, carefully and very finely slice the potatoes. Transfer to a large bowl, drizzle over the olive oil, season generously with salt and toss with your hands to coat well.

Spread out the potato slices in a single layer on the prepared trays, making sure there is no overlap. Roast for 14–16 minutes, or until golden brown and starting to curl. Remove the potato crisps from the oven and immediately season with the chicken salt so it sticks to the residual oil. For ultimate crispiness, transfer the crisps to a wire rack to cool and dry out. Serve and enjoy.

Serves 4

SNACKABLE FACT
Picking the right potato for these crisps can be the difference between crispy and CRISPY. My tip is to go for a waxy variety like red delight, pontiac, yukon gold or kestrel.

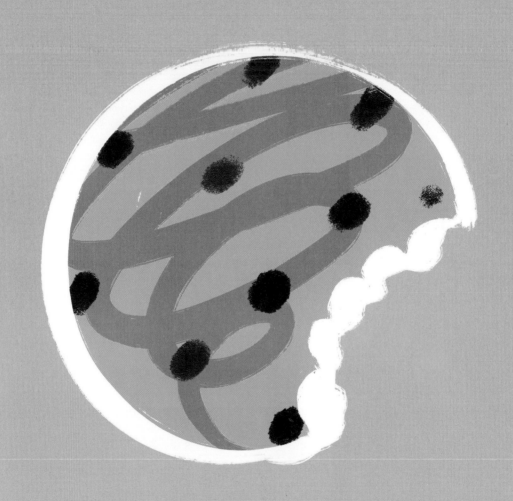

BAKE IT!

MINDFUL EATING

Hands up if you've ever been guilty of making something – could have been a big batch of cookies, a giant brownie or a tray of sweet potato fries – and you told yourself you'd have a normal portion and save the rest for later, but before you know it, you've devoured the entire thing, to the point where you're eating it straight out of the pan? *MY HAND IS UP!* Well, this is when we need to tune back into what our body actually needs – and it doesn't really need an entire tray of brownies, even though they do taste great. For me, mindful eating is when we are in tune with ourselves enough to eat when we are genuinely hungry and know when we are full enough to stop. We can make this process easier by eating nutrient-dense real foods. The snacks in this book have all been chosen to nourish and leave you feeling satisfied. A little goes a long way, meaning: you can have a slice of something now, but have enough leftover for the days ahead. A mindful eater is an empowered eater.

LOW-CARB PUMPKIN AND SEED LOAF

DF GF LC SF

If anybody says you can't enjoy great-tasting bread when going low carb, think again. This is *the* loaf to bake if you're looking for something that satisfies a toast craving without the extra carbs.

Please note: Flax or chia eggs aren't a suitable substitute for eggs in this recipe.

6 eggs
125 ml (½ cup) melted coconut oil
250 g (2 cups) grated butternut pumpkin
135 g (1 cup) grated zucchini
150 g (1½ cups) blanched almond meal
65 g (½ cup) coconut flour
20 g (¼ cup) psyllium husks
70 g (½ cup) pumpkin seeds, plus extra
   1 tablespoon

60 g (½ cup) sunflower seeds, plus extra
   1 tablespoon
1 tablespoon smoked paprika
2 teaspoons garlic powder
2 teaspoons gluten-free baking powder
2 teaspoons sea salt

Preheat the oven to 180°C and grease and line the base and sides of a 20 cm × 8 cm loaf tin with baking paper.

Place the eggs and coconut oil in a large bowl and whisk well to combine. Mix in the pumpkin and zucchini and set aside. In a separate bowl, combine the almond meal, coconut flour, psyllium husks, pumpkin and sunflower seeds, spices, baking powder and salt and mix well.

Add the dry ingredients to the wet ingredients and mix well with a wooden spoon. Pour into the prepared tin and sprinkle over the extra seeds. Bake for 50–60 minutes, or until golden brown on top and a skewer inserted in the centre comes out clean. Allow to cool in the tin for 10 minutes, or until cool enough to handle. Turn the bread out onto a wire rack to cool a little before slicing.

Best enjoyed still warm from the oven or sliced and toasted the next day. Store in an airtight container in the fridge for up to 5 days or freeze for up to 3 months.

Makes 1 loaf

MINI MUSHIE FRITTARTIES

DF GF LC NF SF

Sometimes you need something nutritionally balanced, easy to eat and ready to go when you're running out the door of a morning. Look no further than these mini frittatas. This is the perfect recipe to make in bulk at the start of the week, so you have these on hand for busy-morning breakfasts or snacks on the go.

Please note: Flax or chia eggs aren't a suitable substitute for eggs in this recipe.

2 tablespoons melted butter or coconut oil, or extra-virgin olive oil, for greasing
12 eggs, whisked
1 teaspoon garlic powder
1 teaspoon smoked paprika
sea salt and freshly ground black pepper
1 red onion, finely diced
180 g (2 cups) finely sliced Swiss brown mushrooms
45 g (1 cup) finely chopped baby spinach leaves

12 cherry tomatoes, quartered
1 tablespoon finely chopped flat-leaf parsley leaves
1 teaspoon chilli flakes

AVOCADO SMASH
2 avocados, roughly diced
zest and juice of 1 lime
1 tablespoon apple cider vinegar
½ teaspoon sea salt

Preheat the oven to 180°C and grease a non-stick 12-hole muffin tin with your preferred fat.

Place the whisked egg, garlic powder, paprika and a generous pinch of salt and pepper in a large bowl. Whisk until light and fluffy and well combined, add the onion and whisk briefly to incorporate.

Pour the egg mixture evenly into the prepared muffin tin, then top with the mushroom, spinach, tomato quarters and a pinch of salt. Bake for 20–25 minutes, or until cooked through and lightly golden brown on top. Allow the frittarties to cool slightly in the tin before turning out.

Meanwhile, place the avocado smash ingredients in a bowl and smash together with a fork until rough, rustic and well combined.

Enjoy the frittarties warm with a dollop of avocado smash and a sprinkle of parsley and chilli flakes.

Makes 12

SNACKABLE FACT

This recipe is super versatile, so feel free to mix up your vegetables and spices. Some good swaps and additions include finely chopped red capsicum, grated cheese and bacon pieces.

SNACKABLE FACT

For the best and most golden caramelised top, whisk your preferred liquid sweetener with some melted coconut oil or butter, then halfway through baking, spoon over the top. Trust me, this simple step takes this loaf to the next level.

BANANA AND BLACKBERRY BREAD

DF GF LC* NF SF

It is almost 10 years since I filmed *My Kitchen Rules*! For those who are just catching up, I was a finalist in season 4, and one of the first recipes I practised before going on the show was banana bread. I feel like this loaf is 10 years in the making – and it is by far my best yet.

Please note: Flax or chia eggs aren't a suitable substitute for eggs in this recipe.

3 large overripe bananas
4 large eggs
125 ml (½ cup) maple syrup, honey, coconut nectar, or monk fruit syrup for low carb, plus extra for brushing (optional)
3 tablespoons melted coconut oil

100 g (¾ cup) coconut flour
3 tablespoons arrowroot or tapioca flour
2 teaspoons gluten-free baking powder
1 teaspoon vanilla bean paste or powder
½ teaspoon sea salt
135 g (1 heaped cup) blackberries

Preheat the oven to 180°C and grease and line the base and sides of a 20 cm × 8 cm loaf tin with baking paper. (I find using a smaller tin gives you a taller loaf.)

Mash two bananas in a large bowl, add the eggs and use a whisk to continue to mash and combine well. Add the sweetener and coconut oil and mix with a spoon until incorporated. Add the coconut flour, arrowroot or tapioca flour, baking powder, vanilla and salt and mix well to form a thick, chunky batter. Carefully fold in most of the blackberries, ensuring they stay whole and don't get mashed up; reserve a small handful for the top.

Pour the banana mixture into the prepared loaf tin and smooth the top with the back of the spoon. Slice the remaining banana in half lengthways and lightly press into the batter, then scatter over the reserved blackberries and lightly press them into the batter. Bake for 35–45 minutes, or until the bread is golden brown on top and a skewer inserted in the centre comes out mostly clean. Cool in the tin for 10 minutes. Brush or drizzle with extra sweetener if you like, then turn out onto a chopping board and slice. Store in an airtight container in the fridge for up to 5 days or freeze for up to 3 months.

Makes 1 loaf

CHOC–BLUEBERRY KETO CAKES

DF GF LC* NF SF

Coconut flour is incredibly absorbent, hence the need for high amounts of liquid ingredients such as eggs, coconut oil and coconut cream. It can vary from brand to brand, so if your batter is too wet or dry, follow the instructions below and adapt accordingly.

Please note: Flax or chia eggs aren't a suitable substitute for eggs in this recipe.

12 eggs
250 ml (1 cup) melted coconut oil
125 ml (½ cup) canned coconut cream
250 ml (1 cup) maple syrup, honey, coconut nectar, or monk fruit syrup for low carb
235 g (1⅔ cups) coconut flour

2 teaspoons gluten-free baking powder
1 teaspoon vanilla bean paste or powder
310 g (2 cups) blueberries
250 g (1 cup) chopped dark chocolate (80% cacao minimum or to make your own, see page 40)

Preheat the oven to 180°C and line a 12-hole muffin tin with paper cases.

Place the eggs, coconut oil, coconut cream and sweetener in a large bowl and whisk until well combined. Add the coconut flour, baking powder and vanilla and whisk to form a moist, chunky batter. If it's too wet, add a little more coconut flour; if it's too dry, add a little more coconut oil.

Once you're happy with your batter consistency, fold in the blueberries and chocolate, reserving a few blueberries and chocolate chunks for the top.

Spoon the batter evenly into the prepared muffin tin and scatter over the reserved blueberries and chocolate chunks. Bake for 20–25 minutes, or until golden brown on top and a skewer inserted in the centre of a cake comes out mostly clean.

Carefully remove the cakes from the tin and allow to cool a little on a wire rack. Enjoy warm or store in an airtight container in the fridge for up to 5 days or freeze for up to 1 month.

Makes 12

SNACKABLE FACT

Don't forget with this recipe, and many others, that they can all be made lower carb and/or keto friendly by swapping the maple syrup, honey or coconut nectar for low-carb monk fruit syrup – check out my notes on page 17 for more on this.

CARROT CAKE SQUARES

DF GF LC* SF

SNACKABLE FACT
You'll see that in some of the recipes where I use soaked nuts, I simply state to soak them in boiling water for 15 minutes or so. For this recipe, however, the frosting needs to be silky smooth, hence the much longer soaking time.

Carrot cake is one of those things I love but don't have nearly often enough. If you're like me and also love it, now is the perfect time to whip up this epic recipe.

Please note: Flax or chia eggs aren't a suitable substitute for eggs in this recipe.

8 eggs
250 ml (1 cup) melted coconut oil
zest and juice of 1 lemon
250 ml (1 cup) maple syrup, honey, coconut nectar, or monk fruit syrup for low carb
155 g (2 cups) grated carrot
125 g (1 cup) arrowroot or tapioca flour
130 g (1 cup) coconut flour
2 teaspoons ground cinnamon
2 teaspoons ground nutmeg
2 teaspoons ground ginger
2 teaspoons vanilla bean paste or powder
2 teaspoons gluten-free baking powder

120 g (1 cup) roughly chopped pecans, toasted

LEMON-MACADAMIA FROSTING
320 g (2 cups) raw macadamia nuts, soaked in cold water overnight or boiling water for 2 hours, drained
125 ml (½ cup) maple syrup, honey, coconut nectar, or monk fruit syrup for low carb
125 ml (½ cup) melted coconut oil
125 ml (½ cup) canned coconut cream
zest and juice of 2 lemons
1 teaspoon vanilla bean paste or powder

Preheat the oven to 180°C and grease and line the base and sides of a 20 cm square cake tin with baking paper.

For the lemon-macadamia frosting, place the macadamia nuts, sweetener, coconut oil, coconut cream, lemon zest and juice and vanilla in a food processor and blitz until well combined, smooth and creamy. Pour into a bowl, cover and place in the fridge to chill and firm up for 20 minutes.

While the frosting sets, get on with your cake. Place the eggs, coconut oil, lemon zest and juice and sweetener in a large bowl and whisk until well combined. Stir in the carrot and set aside. In a separate bowl, combine the arrowroot or tapioca flour, coconut flour, spices, vanilla and baking powder and mix well. Pour the dry ingredients into the wet ingredients and mix well to form a thick, chunky batter. If it's too wet, add a little more coconut flour; if it's too dry, add a little more coconut oil. Fold through half the pecans.

Pour the batter into the prepared tin and bake for 30-40 minutes, or until the cake is golden brown on top and a skewer inserted in the centre comes out mostly clean. Allow to cool slightly before turning out onto a wire rack to cool completely.

Take the frosting out of the fridge and slather all over the carrot cake. Sprinkle over the remaining pecans and cut into nine squares to serve. Store in an airtight container in the fridge for up to 5 days or freeze for up to 1 month.

Makes 9

BAKE IT!

MUFFINS

I am obsessed with muffins, and once you master the base recipe, any flavour combination is possible. Here is a guide to creating your own epic combo.

When experimenting with different ingredients it's important to be intuitive. If your muffin batter is too dry or crumbly, add more binder or oil to get it moving; if it's too wet, add more of your chosen base to thicken it up.

Depending on what combo you create, your muffins can be DF, GF, LC, NF, PB or SF.

Non-negotiables	
Sweetener	Flavourings
Binder	Fruit
Crunch	Soft fruit or veg
Base	

BASE
3 cups

almond meal
hazelnut meal
macadamia nut meal

THE NON-NEGOTIABLES
for any combo

1 teaspoon gluten-free baking powder
1 teaspoon apple cider vinegar
½ teaspoon sea salt

CRUNCH
½ cup

cacao nibs
roughly chopped nuts
shredded coconut
toasted seeds

BINDER
4 ×

eggs
flax or chia eggs (see page 17)

FLAVOURINGS (OPTIONAL)
1 teaspoon

ground cinnamon,
ginger or nutmeg
lemon or orange zest
vanilla bean paste or powder

SWEETENER
3 tablespoons

coconut nectar
honey
maple syrup
monk fruit syrup

SOFT FRUIT OR VEG
½ cup

apple sauce
mashed banana
pumpkin puree

GOOD OIL
3 tablespoons

avocado oil
coconut oil
extra-virgin olive oil
macadamia nut oil

FRUIT (OPTIONAL)
1 cup

blackberries
blueberries
diced apple
diced pineapple
raspberries
strawberries

METHOD

Preheat the oven to 180°C and line a 12-hole muffin tin with paper cases.

Combine your base, crunch, baking powder, salt and spice (if using) in a large bowl, mix well and make a well in the centre. In a separate bowl, whisk together your binder, soft fruit or veg, sweetener, oil and apple cider vinegar. Pour the wet ingredients into the dry ingredients and mix well with a wooden spoon or spatula. Stir in the fruit (if using) until combined.

Spoon the batter evenly into the prepared muffin tin and bake for 15–20 minutes, or until the muffins are golden brown on top and a skewer inserted in the centre comes out clean.

Allow the muffins to cool slightly before removing from the tin and enjoying. Store in an airtight container in the fridge for up to 5 days or freeze for up to 3 months.

Makes 12

VERY GOOD VANILLA
SLICE SLAB

DF GF LC* SF

SNACKABLE FACT

You can find low-carb keto versions of most traditional sugars these days. One of my favourites is monk fruit icing sugar – it works and tastes just like the real thing, and is perfect to top this vanilla slice.

Is it just me or does every small town across Australia claim to have *the* best vanilla slice? Look, no disrespect to them because they are all delicious, but you can make your own without the fuss of making puff pastry – and now you, too, can put up a sign out the front of your house saying 'home of the best vanilla slice'.

3 tablespoons monk fruit icing
    sugar (optional)

BASE
225 g (1½ cups) raw macadamia nuts
    or cashew nuts, lightly toasted
135 g (1½ cups) desiccated coconut,
    lightly toasted
125 ml (½ cup) maple syrup, honey, coconut
    nectar, or monk fruit syrup for low carb
125 ml (½ cup) melted butter or coconut oil
2 teaspoons vanilla bean paste or powder

VANILLA CUSTARD
750 ml (3 cups) canned coconut cream
2 teaspoons vanilla bean paste or powder
4 egg yolks
1 tablespoon arrowroot or tapioca flour
125 ml (½ cup) maple syrup, honey, coconut
    nectar, or monk fruit syrup for low carb
2 tablespoons gelatine powder
3 tablespoons boiling water

Line a 20 cm square cake tin with baking paper.

For the base, combine the macadamias or cashews, desiccated coconut, sweetener, butter or coconut oil and vanilla in a food processor and blitz until a sticky crumb forms that holds together when pressed with your fingers.

Tip the base mixture into the prepared tin and use your fingers to smooth, flatten and press it into the edges. Transfer to the fridge or freezer to set for 20-30 minutes while you start on your custard.

For the vanilla custard, place the coconut cream and vanilla in a saucepan over medium-low heat and, whisking constantly, bring just to a simmer for about 5-6 minutes. Remove from the heat. Combine the egg yolks, arrowroot or tapioca flour and sweetener in a bowl and whisk well. Whisk in the hot coconut cream until well incorporated. Place the gelatine powder and boiling water in a small heatproof bowl, stir to dissolve the gelatine, then slowly whisk into the coconut cream mixture. Place the pan over very low heat and cook, whisking frequently, for 25–30 minutes, or until the custard is lovely and thick, silky and creamy. Be mindful to watch the heat and keep the custard moving so it doesn't burn or curdle. Set aside to cool for 20-30 minutes.

Pour the cooled custard over the base, cover and place in the fridge to set for 6-8 hours or overnight.

Once the vanilla slice slab is firm, cut into nine squares with a warm knife, dipped in hot water between slices. Sift over the monk fruit powder (if using) and serve. Store in an airtight container in the fridge for up to 5 days or freeze for up to 1 month.

Makes 9

SALTED BROWNIE BISCUITS

DF GF SF

In my opinion, a brownie should be the perfect balance between sticky, fudgy and chewy, with a lovely textured top and rich chocolate flavour. Well, if that sounds like your cup of tea, be sure to try these biscuits – I have captured all that and more in each and every bite.

330 g (1½ cups) cacao butter
125 ml (½ cup) melted coconut oil
125 ml (½ cup) maple syrup
250 g (2 cups) cacao powder
150 g (1½ cups) blanched almond meal
185 g (1½ cups) arrowroot or tapioca flour
90 g (½ cup) coconut sugar

2 teaspoons vanilla bean paste or powder
1 teaspoon gluten-free baking powder
500 g (2 cups) dark chocolate chips
    (80% cacao minimum or to make your
    own, see page 40)
sea salt flakes
2 eggs, whisked

Heat the cacao butter and coconut oil in a saucepan over medium–low heat, whisking to combine. Add the maple syrup and cacao powder and whisk until smooth. Remove from the heat and set aside to cool.

Meanwhile, place the almond meal, arrowroot or tapioca flour, coconut sugar, vanilla, baking powder, chocolate chips and a generous pinch of salt in a large bowl, mix well and set aside.

Once the cacao butter mixture is cool, pour into the dry ingredients and mix well. Add the whisked egg and mix to form a wet, workable dough.

Roll the dough into a ball, cover with plastic wrap and chill in the fridge for at least 2 hours or, even better, overnight. This is very important; we don't want the biscuits to melt when they are in the oven.

When it's time to bake, preheat the oven to 180°C and line a baking tray with baking paper.

Working quickly, roll 2 tablespoons of dough per biscuit into balls and place on the prepared tray, allowing room for spreading. Press down lightly on each ball and bake for 10–12 minutes, or until just cooked. You want the biscuits to be a little bit sticky.

Allow the biscuits to cool on the tray a little before enjoying while still warm. These biscuits are even better with a pinch of salt sprinkled on top. Store in an airtight container in the fridge for up to 5 days or freeze for up to 1 month.

Makes about 15

SNACKABLE FACT

Coconut sugar is one of my favourite sweeteners to use in biscuits because of the rich caramelised flavour it brings to baking – it's like the healthier version of a rich dark brown sugar.

GOLDEN CHOCADAMIA COOKIES

DF GF LC SF

I often experiment with different flavours, but one tried-and-true combination I keep coming back to is dark chocolate and macadamia nuts. There is something about the bitterness of the chocolate and the butteriness of the macadamia nuts that wins me over every time, and with a hint of salt, you really can't go wrong.

2 eggs
185 g (1 cup) coconut sugar
125 ml (½ cup) melted butter or coconut oil
200 g (2 cups) blanched almond meal
250 g (2 cups) arrowroot or tapioca flour
1 teaspoon vanilla bean paste or powder
1 teaspoon gluten-free baking powder

½ teaspoon sea salt
160 g (1 cup) roughly chopped macadamia nuts, lightly toasted
250 g (1 cup) chopped dark chocolate (80% cacao minimum or to make your own, see page 40)

Place the eggs, coconut sugar and butter or coconut oil in a bowl and whisk well to form a wet, sticky golden paste. The coconut sugar will break down and become caramel-like. Add the almond meal, arrowroot or tapioca flour, vanilla, baking powder and salt and mix until completely incorporated to form a wet, workable and chunky dough. If the dough is too wet, add a little more almond meal; if it's too dry, add a little more melted butter or coconut oil.

Once you're happy with the dough, fold through the macadamia nuts and chocolate. Cover the bowl with plastic wrap and transfer to the fridge for 15–30 minutes to firm up.

Preheat the oven to 180°C and line two baking trays with baking paper.

Divide the dough into 10 to 12 evenly sized portions, roll into balls and place on the prepared trays, allowing room for spreading. Bake for 10–12 minutes, or until the cookies are golden brown and cooked through. Allow to cool and crisp up nicely on the trays before serving. Store in an airtight container in the fridge for up to 5 days or freeze for up to 1 month.

Makes 10–12

MINI SPICED PUMPKIN SAUSAGE ROLLS

DF GF LC SF

I am mad for sausage rolls. Absolutely mad! When I see a bakery that claims to have the best sausage rolls, I am all over it – and I can't just have one, I need to try the entire range. This recipe combines pumpkin and lamb, two of my favourite flavours. Served alongside your favourite sauces and accompaniments, you really can't go wrong.

200 g fatty lamb mince
½ small red onion, finely diced
1 garlic clove, grated
2 teaspoons curry powder
1 teaspoon chilli flakes
½ teaspoon ground cumin
½ teaspoon ground coriander
125 g (1 cup) finely grated
   butternut pumpkin

sea salt and freshly ground black pepper
1 egg, separated
1 tablespoon sesame seeds

GOLDEN PASTRY
200 g (2 cups) blanched almond meal
3 tablespoons melted butter
2 eggs, whisked
1 teaspoon gluten-free baking powder

Preheat the oven to 170°C and line two baking trays with baking paper.

For the golden pastry, combine the almond meal, butter, whisked egg and baking powder in a bowl and mix well to form a sticky, wet dough. You should be able to roll it so it holds its form without cracking or breaking apart. If it's too dry, add a little more melted butter; if it's too wet, add a little more almond meal. Roll into four evenly sized balls, cover with plastic wrap and chill in the fridge for 20–30 minutes while you get started on the filling.

Combine the lamb mince, onion, garlic, curry powder, chilli flakes, cumin, coriander, pumpkin and a generous pinch of salt and pepper in a large bowl. Mix well with your hands until all the flavours are incorporated. Add the egg white and mix until the mixture feels sticky and starts to bind.

Remove a dough ball from the fridge and place it on a sheet of baking paper. Cover with another sheet of baking paper and roll out the dough to form a 10 cm × 15 cm rectangle about 5 mm thick. Place a quarter of the filling in a log shape down the middle of the dough. Fold the dough over the filling to enclose it. Whisk the egg yolk in a small bowl and, using a pastry brush, brush a little along the seam and press down lightly to seal. Slice the roll crossways into three. Repeat with the remaining balls of dough and filling. Place the sausage rolls, seam-side down, on the prepared trays.

Brush a little egg yolk over the top of each sausage roll (this egg wash helps them turn golden brown) and sprinkle on the sesame seeds. Bake for 25–30 minutes, or until the pastry is golden brown and the filling is cooked through. Best enjoyed on the day of baking.

Makes 12

CINNAMON DOUGHNUT BITES

GF SF

I don't know anyone who doesn't walk past a doughnut shop and take a deep breath in, devouring all the incredible smells from freshly baked hot cinnamon doughnuts. Now you can not only enjoy that smell, but the incredible taste too, in the comfort of your home.

120 g unsalted butter or 120 ml coconut oil
pinch of sea salt
100 g (1 cup) almond meal
100 g (¾ cup) arrowroot or tapioca flour
½ teaspoon gluten-free baking powder

3 eggs
coconut oil, for deep-frying
1 tablespoon ground cinnamon
200 g (1 cup) super-fine coconut sugar

Add the butter or oil, salt and 250 ml (1 cup) of water to a large saucepan and bring to the boil over medium heat. Using a wooden spoon, stir in the almond meal, tapioca flour and baking powder and mix together well to form a smooth, ball-shaped dough. Transfer to a bowl and set aside to cool.

Once cool, transfer the dough to the bowl of a stand mixer fitted with a paddle attachment. On medium speed, add the eggs one at a time, beating until incorporated after each addition. Set aside in the fridge for 30 minutes to rest, then spoon the dough into a piping bag fitted with a 2 cm round nozzle or a zip-lock bag with a hole snipped in one of the bottom corners.

Half-fill a heavy-based saucepan with coconut oil and set over medium heat. Heat the oil to 180°C. To test if it is hot enough, simply drop a small piece of the dough into the oil – if it sizzles and bubbles, you're good to go.

Using a small, sharp knife to cut the dough, pipe six to eight 3–4 cm balls into the oil. Deep-fry for 1–2 minutes, until golden brown. Remove the balls using a heat-safe slotted spoon and transfer to paper towel to drain. Repeat with the remaining dough, being mindful not to overcrowd the pan.

Combine the cinnamon and coconut sugar in a shallow bowl.

To serve, toss the doughnut bites in the cinnamon–sugar mixture, arrange in a bowl and devour.

SERVES 4–6

FAKE
IT!

MY CLASSIC
RE-CREATIONS OF
FAMILY FAVOURITES
THAT TASTE JUST
LIKE THE REAL
THING

DON'T CUT IT, SWAP IT

I've never been a believer in cutting out favourite foods. It's not sustainable long term, nor is it very fun. Imagine if I told you right now you could never ever have your most favourite food ever again? You'd not only be really sad, you'd either be really miserable and crave it, or crack under the cravings and devour 10 times more than you'd ordinarily eat. My approach to sustainable healthy eating? Don't cut it, swap it. By making healthier versions of your favourite foods, you'll still get to enjoy that same great taste without any of the traditional nasties. And hitting that craving on the head means you won't binge or feel as though you're going without. I love that my week's food is really varied: I have a curry some nights, pasta other nights, even pizza and fish and chips. But how can I do this? What's the key? They're my nutrient-dense versions – so I can have my faves as often as I like without compromising my health and wellness goals. Life would be pretty boring without cake, right?

FAKE IT!

BANANA PIKELETS

DF GF NF SF

Pikelets are pretty much just delicious mini pancakes, and the good news is because they're smaller, you can have more. Whip up a massive stack of these and you will think all your snack dreams have come true.

2 ripe bananas, roughly chopped
4 eggs
120 g (1 cup) arrowroot or tapioca flour
3 tablespoons maple syrup, honey or
    coconut nectar, plus extra to serve

1 teaspoon vanilla bean paste or powder
1 teaspoon gluten-free baking powder
2 tablespoons butter or coconut oil
125 g (½ cup) vanilla bean coconut yoghurt
80 g (½ cup) fresh or frozen blueberries

Preheat the oven to 120°C.

Place the banana, eggs, arrowroot or tapioca flour, sweetener, vanilla and baking powder in a large bowl and blitz with a hand-held blender until smooth and thick and the batter is a lovely dolloping consistency.

Melt some of the butter or coconut oil in a large frying pan over medium–high heat. Cooking three or four pikelets at a time, drop a ladle of batter per pikelet into the pan and cook for 3-4 minutes, or until small bubbles appear on top and the pikelets are firm enough to turn. Flip and continue to cook until both sides are golden brown and the pikelets are cooked through. Transfer to a plate and place in the oven to keep warm. Repeat until you have 16 pikelets in total.

To serve, stack your pikelets on each serving plate, top with the coconut yoghurt and blueberries and enjoy.

Serves 4

SNACKABLE FACT

If you're short on time or ingredients, this also works as a simple three-ingredient recipe: just use the banana, eggs and flour, blitz and you're good to go. They taste great!

SNACKABLE
FACT
This recipe also works
really well with sweet
potato and zucchini, so
try each individually or
a combination of both.

POPCORN CHICKEN NUGGETS

DF GF LC SF

Once you pop you just can't stop! These popcorn chicken nuggets have the perfect balance of spice with a good level of heat. If the little ones aren't fans of chilli, you can simply omit it.

600 g chicken mince
1 tablespoon arrowroot or tapioca flour
2 teaspoons garlic powder
1 teaspoon onion powder
1 teaspoon smoked paprika
1 teaspoon cayenne pepper
1 teaspoon chilli flakes
1 teaspoon dried oregano
1 egg, whisked
sea salt
extra-virgin olive oil cooking spray
Chilli-lime Aioli (see page 97), to serve

CRUMB
2 egg whites, whisked
60 g (½ cup) arrowroot or tapioca flour
60 g (½ cup) blanched almond meal
3 tablespoons desiccated coconut
2 tablespoons white chia seeds
1 tablespoon smoked paprika
½ teaspoon sea salt

Preheat the oven to 180°C and line a baking tray with baking paper.

Place the chicken mince, arrowroot or tapioca flour, spices, egg and 1 teaspoon of salt in a bowl and mix well with your hands to combine. You should have a sticky mixture that holds its form and can be rolled into small balls. If it's too wet, add a little more arrowroot or tapioca flour; if it's too dry, add another egg. Working with 1 heaped teaspoon of mixture at a time, roll into balls and place on a large plate.

To start on the crumb, set up three shallow bowls for a crumbing station. Add the whisked egg white to one bowl, place the arrowroot or tapioca flour in another and combine the almond meal, desiccated coconut, chia seeds, paprika and salt in the third bowl.

Roll each ball in the arrowroot or tapioca flour, dip in the egg wash, then coat with the almond meal crumb mixture. Place each crumbed ball on the prepared tray and spray with the olive oil so you have nice even coverage. Bake for 10–12 minutes, or until the nuggets are golden brown on the outside and cooked through. Serve hot with the chilli–lime aioli.

Serves 4

FAST FISH FINGERS

DF GF LC SF

Fish fingers always remind me of a weekend snack I used to have as a kid. Now you can make your own really easily and quickly and, knowing they are packed with goodness, enjoy the same great flavour.

2 eggs, lightly whisked
100 g (1 cup) blanched almond meal
45 g (½ cup) desiccated coconut
60 g (½ cup) arrowroot or tapioca flour
3 tablespoons finely chopped flat-leaf
    parsley leaves
1 teaspoon onion powder
1 teaspoon garlic powder
1 teaspoon smoked paprika
½ teaspoon sea salt
400 g firm white fish, cut into fingers
    about 10 cm long

extra-virgin olive oil, avocado or macadamia
    oil cooking spray
dressed green salad, to serve
lemon wedges, to serve

ONE-MINUTE LEMONY MAYO
250 ml (1 cup) extra-virgin olive oil
1 egg
1 teaspoon freshly squeezed lemon juice,
    plus extra if needed
½ teaspoon dijon mustard
pinch of sea salt

For the one-minute lemony mayo, pour the extra-virgin olive oil into a wide-mouthed glass jar – a mason jar works really well for this. Add the egg and let it settle for a moment (this helps the mayo to emulsify). Insert a hand-held blender and press it down to the bottom of the jar, making sure you pierce the egg yolk. Turn on the blender and keep it at the bottom of the jar for 30 seconds, or until the mixture at the bottom is emulsified and a pale creamy colour. Now, taking your time, very gradually lift the blender up to emulsify more of the oil. Slowly continue all the way to the top until all the oil is thickened, emulsified and nice and creamy. Stir in the lemon juice, mustard and salt. Taste and add more lemon, if you like. Screw on the lid and store in the fridge for up to 1 week, ready for serving.

Preheat the oven to 200°C and line a large baking tray with baking paper.

Set up two shallow bowls for a crumbing station. Add the whisked egg to one bowl, combine the almond meal, desiccated coconut, arrowroot or tapioca flour, parsley, spices and salt in the other bowl and mix well. Dunk the fish fingers in the egg, then coat in the crumb and place on the prepared tray. Generously spray with the cooking oil and bake for 10–12 minutes, turning halfway through, until golden brown and cooked through.

Serve the fish fingers hot from the oven with a green salad, lemon wedges and a generous dollop of the lemony mayo.

Serves 2

SNACKABLE FACT

This lemony mayo recipe uses the hand-held blender technique. If you don't have one, you can use a small food processor or blender. Blitz together the oil and egg until smooth, emulsified and a pale creamy colour. Add the lemon juice, mustard and salt and blitz again until completely combined. Pour into a glass jar with a lid and store in the fridge until needed.

BEEF CURRY BITES

DF GF LC NF SF

I have curries a few nights a week, usually a butter chicken one day and a beef curry another. Red curry is a favourite for beef. The curry paste is really simple to make from scratch but, equally, you can find really good pre-made ones at most supermarkets. Here, those flavours come together in perfect snack form.

400 g beef mince
3 tablespoons arrowroot or tapioca flour
2 garlic cloves, finely chopped
1 long red chilli, finely diced
1 tablespoon grated ginger
1 teaspoon chilli flakes
2 eggs
sea salt
2 tablespoons extra-virgin olive oil
    or coconut oil

2 tablespoons Thai red curry paste
1 tablespoon coconut aminos or tamari
1 tablespoon tomato paste
125 ml (½ cup) beef bone broth or stock
250 ml (1 cup) canned coconut cream
3 tablespoons shredded coconut, toasted
3 tablespoons coriander leaves
lime cheeks, to serve

Place the beef mince, arrowroot or tapioca flour, garlic, chilli, ginger, chilli flakes, eggs and a pinch of salt in a bowl and mix well with your hands to combine. Roll into 12 evenly sized meatballs and place on a plate.

Heat the olive or coconut oil in a large frying pan over medium–high heat, add the meatballs and cook, turning regularly, for 6–8 minutes, or until golden brown on all sides. Carefully transfer the meatballs to a plate and set aside while you make the sauce.

To the same pan, add the curry paste, coconut aminos or tamari and tomato paste and fry, stirring occasionally, for 1–2 minutes, or until aromatic. Pour in the broth or stock and coconut cream and bring to a simmer. Cook, stirring, for 4–5 minutes, or until the sauce is thickened.

Return the meatballs to the pan and simmer for 4–5 minutes, or until the meatballs are cooked through and the sauce is very thick.

Arrange the beef curry bites on a platter, scatter over the shredded coconut and coriander, add a generous squeeze of lime juice and serve with the lime cheeks on the side.

Serves 3–4

CHOCOLATE FUDGE

I'm known for my raw chocolate creations, so I had to share my go-to tips for homemade fudgy chocolate snacks. This ultimate guide will help you create your own favourite flavour combo.

Follow the outline below and for each component feel free to use one element straight up or try a combo of a few to make your perfect blend.

When experimenting with different ingredients it's important to be intuitive. If your chocolate is a bit too thick, add some cacao butter or coconut oil; if it's too runny, add some cacao powder, nut butter or sweetener to thicken it up.

Depending on what combo you create, your chocolate fudge can be DF, GF, LC, NF, PB or SF.

Extras

Sweetener

Nut butter

Base

Chocolate base

BASE
I cup

cacao butter
coconut oil

CHOCOLATE BASE
250 g (2 cups)

cacao powder

NUT BUTTER
I cup

coconut butter
macadamia nut butter
smooth peanut butter

SWEETENER
½ cup

coconut nectar
honey
maple syrup
monk fruit syrup

EXTRAS (OPTIONAL)

cayenne pepper
chilli powder
dried fruit
edible essential lemon oil
edible essential lime oil
edible essential orange oil
edible essential peppermint oil
ground cinnamon
rosewater
sea salt flakes
shredded coconut
toasted hazelnuts
toasted macadamia nuts
toasted pecans
toasted pistachio nuts
vanilla bean paste or powder

METHOD

Line a 20 cm square cake tin with baking paper, or line a standard 12-hole muffin tin with paper cases.

Place your preferred base in a saucepan over medium-low heat and melt, stirring occasionally. Add the nut butter, reduce the heat to low and cook, stirring frequently, for 3–4 minutes, or until the nut butter has softened and is completely incorporated. Remove the pan from the heat and gently whisk in the cacao power and sweetener of your choice. Keep whisking until thick, creamy and well combined, then taste and evaluate the consistency and sweetness as follows:

- For a thicker, darker chocolate, add more cacao powder.

- For a smoother chocolate, add more coconut oil.

- For a fudgier chocolate, add more nut butter.

- For a sweeter chocolate, add more sweetener.

Once you're happy with your base, stir in your preferred optional extras. Some of my favourite combos include a pinch of salt and toasted pistachio nuts; vanilla and macadamia nuts; or a mixed nut and dried fruit rocky road. Pour the mixture into the prepared tin, then transfer to the freezer for 20 minutes, or until firm.

Remove the fudge from the freezer. If using the cake tin, lift out the fudge by pulling on the edges of the baking paper. Using a hot knife, cut the fudge into diamonds or squares. If using the muffin tin, turn out the muffins. Enjoy immediately.

Store leftovers in an airtight container in the fridge for up to 2 weeks or freeze for up to 3 months. The chocolate fudge is best served chilled straight from the fridge.

Makes about 500 g

FAKE IT!

CHOCOLATE CRACKLE SLAB

DF GF LC* NF* PB SF

When we were kids, was it even a real birthday party if there weren't chocolate crackles? This recipe is a next-level way to enjoy that moreish flavour and crunch, but with the added nutritional benefits of healthy ingredients.

110 g (½ cup) cacao butter
135 g (½ cup) crunchy peanut butter
125 ml (½ cup) maple syrup, coconut nectar, or monk fruit syrup for low carb
60 g (½ cup) cacao powder

60 g (1 cup) shredded coconut
120 g (1 cup) roughly chopped pecans
20 g (1 cup) buckwheat puffs or extra shredded coconut (optional)
1 teaspoon vanilla bean paste or powder

Line a 20 cm square baking tin with baking paper.

Melt the cacao butter in a saucepan over medium–low heat. Stir in the peanut butter and sweetener, remove from the heat and set aside.

Combine the cacao powder, shredded coconut, pecans, buckwheat puffs (if using) and vanilla in a large bowl and mix well. Make a well in the centre.

Pour the wet ingredients into the dry ingredients and mix well with a wooden spoon or spatula.

Spoon the mixture into the prepared tin and transfer to the fridge to set for 30 minutes.

Remove the chocolate crackle slab from the fridge and cut into your desired serving shape and size. Enjoy at once or store in an airtight container in the fridge for up to 1 week or freeze for up to 3 months.

Serves 12–14

LUKEY'S LEMON TART

DF GF LC* NF SF

There isn't a better flavour combination than golden brown pastry and extra zesty and tart lemon curd. If you use monk fruit syrup in this recipe, it becomes low carb and keto friendly, too.

CRUST
2 eggs
170 ml (⅔ cup) melted butter or coconut oil
80 ml (⅓ cup) maple syrup, or maple-
    flavoured monk fruit syrup for low carb
130 g (1 cup) coconut flour
½ teaspoon sea salt

LEMON CURD FILLING
4 eggs
4 egg yolks
250 ml (1 cup) maple syrup, or maple-
    flavoured monk fruit syrup for low carb
250 ml (1 cup) freshly squeezed lemon juice
zest of 4 lemons
170 ml (⅔ cup) melted coconut oil
pinch of sea salt

TO SERVE
250 g (1 cup) vanilla bean coconut yoghurt
    or coconut cream
finely grated zest of 1 lemon

Preheat the oven to 200°C and grease a shallow 24 cm fluted tart tin with a removable base.

For the crust, place the eggs, butter or coconut oil and sweetener in a bowl and whisk until smooth and incorporated. Add the coconut flour and salt and mix well with a spoon or spatula to make a thick, sticky and wet dough.

Use your hands to press the dough into the base and edge and up the side, right to the top of the tin. You want the thickness to be fairly even all over for consistent baking. Prick the pastry with a fork and bake for 8–10 minutes, or until golden brown. Set aside to cool.

Place the lemon curd filling ingredients in a saucepan and whisk over low heat until smooth and combined. Gradually increase the heat to medium and cook, whisking constantly, for 10–15 minutes, or until the curd thickens and coats the back of a spoon. (You want to keep the curd moving so it doesn't stick and catch on the bottom of the pan.) To make sure it's completely smooth, press the curd through a fine sieve, then pour over the crust.

Transfer the tart to the fridge for 2 hours or so until the lemon curd is completely firm. Remove the tart from the tin, cut into slices and serve with a dollop of coconut yoghurt or coconut cream and a sprinkle of lemon zest.

Serves 12

FAKE IT!

THE MARZ BAR

DF* GF LC* NF* PB SF

As the old saying goes: 'a Mars a day helps you work, rest and play'. And that couldn't be more true when it comes to this version. I've swapped out the refined sugars and processed ingredients for nutrient-dense alternatives that give you the same great taste.

NOUGAT
270 g (1 cup) smooth peanut butter, or tahini for nut free
250 ml (1 cup) maple syrup, coconut nectar, or maple-flavoured monk fruit syrup for low carb
250 ml (1 cup) canned coconut cream
130 g (1 cup) coconut flour
70 g (½ cup) coconut sugar, or granulated monk fruit sweetener for low carb
60 g (½ cup) cacao powder
1 teaspoon vanilla bean paste or powder

CARAMEL
270 g (1 cup) smooth peanut butter, or tahini for nut free
250 ml (1 cup) maple syrup, coconut nectar, or maple-flavoured monk fruit syrup for low carb
250 ml (1 cup) melted butter, or coconut oil for dairy free

CHOCOLATE LAYER
220 g (1 cup) cacao butter
125 g (1 cup) cacao powder
125 ml (½ cup) maple syrup, coconut nectar, or maple-flavoured monk fruit syrup for low carb
1 teaspoon vanilla bean paste or powder

Line a 20 cm square cake tin with baking paper.

For the nougat, combine the peanut butter or tahini, liquid sweetener and coconut cream in a large bowl and mix with a spoon until smooth and incorporated. Add the coconut flour, granulated sweetener, cacao powder and vanilla and mix well. If the nougat is a little dry, add some more coconut cream; if it's too wet, add a touch more coconut flour. Press into the base of the prepared tin with your hands and transfer to the fridge or freezer to firm up while you get on with the caramel.

Place the caramel ingredients in a saucepan over medium–low heat and whisk until thick, smooth and creamy. Remove from the heat and pour over the nougat base. Transfer to the fridge to set for 30 minutes.

For the chocolate layer, melt the cacao butter in a saucepan over medium–low heat, then whisk in the cacao powder, sweetener and vanilla until nice and smooth. Remove from the heat and set aside to thicken for 10–15 minutes.

Once the base layers have set, remove from the tin and slice into 10 to 12 bars. Dip the bars in the chocolate to coat well, then place on a wire rack set over a tray to catch the drips. Return to the fridge to set for 10–15 minutes before serving. Store in an airtight container in the fridge for up to 2 weeks or freeze for up to 3 months.

Makes 10–12

FAKE IT!

HINESEY'S HEDGEHOG SLICE

DF GF LC* PB SF

Growing up, one of my all-time fave snacks was a chunky piece of hedgehog slice. With the first bite of this chocolate cookie crunch, I am transported back to my childhood and every mouthful is like a little nostalgia trip.

250 g (1 cup) Chocolate (see page 40)

COOKIE DOUGH
100 g (1 cup) blanched almond meal
90 g (1 cup) desiccated coconut
3 tablespoons maple syrup, honey or
    coconut nectar
250 ml (1 cup) melted coconut oil
1 teaspoon vanilla bean paste or powder
½ teaspoon sea salt

CHOCOLATE BASE
250 ml (1 cup) maple syrup, coconut nectar,
    or monk fruit syrup for low carb
90 g (1 cup) desiccated coconut
100 g (1 cup) pecans
120 g (1 cup) cacao powder
3 tablespoons melted coconut oil
1 teaspoon vanilla bean paste or powder

Line a 21 cm × 11 cm loaf tin with baking paper.

For the cookie dough, place the almond meal and desiccated coconut in a bowl and mix well. Add the sweetener, coconut oil, vanilla and salt and mix to form a slightly sticky dough that holds together. Set aside in the fridge to firm up slightly while you get on with the chocolate base.

Combine the chocolate base ingredients in a large bowl and mix until well incorporated.

Divide the cookie dough into small handfuls, then gently fold them into the chocolate base with your hands until incorporated but still in chunks. Tip into the prepared tin, press to flatten the top and transfer to the fridge to set for 30 minutes.

Meanwhile, prepare the chocolate and set aside to cool slightly.

Pour the melted cooled chocolate over the chocolate cookie dough base and return to the fridge to set for 10-15 minutes.

Turn out the hedgehog slice onto a chopping board and cut into eight to 10 slices. Serve or store in an airtight container in the fridge for up to 2 weeks or freeze for up to 3 months.

Serves 8–10

FAKE IT!

ONE-PAN
WESTERN WHEEL

DF GF LC* SF

As the slogan on the ad once went: 'Eat the wagon wheel!'. Well, now you can as often as you like, because my version is as good for you as it tastes.

250 g (1 cup) Chocolate (see page 40)

BISCUIT BASE
2 eggs
3 tablespoons maple syrup, coconut nectar, or monk fruit syrup for low carb
3 tablespoons melted coconut oil
3 tablespoons canned coconut cream
100 g (1 cup) blanched almond meal
60 g (½ cup) arrowroot or tapioca flour
1 teaspoon vanilla bean paste or powder
1 teaspoon gluten-free baking powder

MARSHMALLOW
250 ml (1 cup) filtered water
1 tablespoon gelatine powder
125 ml (½ cup) maple syrup, coconut nectar, or monk fruit syrup for low carb

RASPBERRY CHIA JAM
1 tablespoon gelatine powder
3 tablespoons cold filtered water
250 g (2 cups) fresh or frozen and thawed raspberries
1 tablespoon chia seeds

Preheat the oven to 180°C. Line a 20 cm square, deep cake tin with baking paper.

For the biscuit base, place the eggs, sweetener, coconut oil and coconut cream in a large bowl and whisk well until smooth. Add the almond meal, arrowroot or tapioca flour, vanilla and baking powder and mix until well combined. Pour into the prepared tin, then spread out and press with your fingers to create an even base. Bake for 10 minutes, or until lightly golden brown on top. Set aside to cool.

Meanwhile, for the marshmallow, combine the water and gelatine in a saucepan over medium–low heat and whisk well to dissolve the gelatine. Remove from the heat, then whisk in the sweetener. Continue to whisk with a hand-held mixer on high for 6–8 minutes, or until the mixture turns white and thickens enough to form soft peaks. Pour over the biscuit base, cover the tin with plastic wrap and transfer to the freezer for 1 hour to set completely.

For the raspberry chia jam, place the gelatine in a small bowl, add the water and allow the mixture to bloom for 5 minutes. Combine the raspberries and chia seeds in a small saucepan over medium–low heat and stir in the gelatine liquid. Cook, stirring, until the raspberries have broken down and the mixture is quite thick and jammy. Set aside to cool to room temperature.

Remove the marshmallow and biscuit base from the freezer, pour over the jam and return to the freezer for 1–2 hours, or until firm but not frozen.

Meanwhile, prepare the chocolate and set aside to cool slightly. Pour the cooled chocolate over the western wheel base and place in the fridge for 15–20 minutes to firm up.

To serve, remove the western wheel slab from the tin and use a hot knife to slice into your preferred portions. Store in an airtight container in the fridge for up to 1 week or freeze for up to 1 month.

Serves 10–12

FAKE IT!

CHERRY DELIGHT

DF GF LC* NF PB SF

This is my healthy take on a Cherry Ripe bar. I love how simple it is – just two elements and no baking required. If cherries aren't your thing, feel free to swap them for blueberries or raspberries, both work really well.

400 g fresh pitted or frozen and
    thawed cherries
180 g (2 cups) desiccated coconut
250 ml (1 cup) maple syrup, coconut nectar,
    or monk fruit syrup for low carb

3 tablespoons melted coconut oil, warm
2 teaspoons vanilla bean paste or powder
220 g (1 cup) cacao butter
125 g (1 cup) cacao powder

Line a 20 cm square cake tin and a baking tray with baking paper.

Place the cherries, desiccated coconut and half the sweetener in a food processor and blitz to form a thick, chunky paste. Add the warm coconut oil and 1 teaspoon of vanilla and pulse to combine well.

Press the cherry mixture into the prepared cake tin and flatten and spread all the way to the edges with your hands. Transfer to the freezer for 30 minutes to chill and firm up.

Meanwhile, melt the cacao butter in a saucepan over medium-low heat. Whisk in the cacao powder, the remaining sweetener and vanilla until incorporated and nice and smooth. Remove from the heat and set aside to thicken.

Slice the cherry layer into six to eight bars, then dunk into the melted chocolate to coat completely. Place the coated bars on the prepared baking tray and return to the freezer for 5-10 minutes, or until the chocolate has set completely. Enjoy straight away or store in an airtight container in the fridge for up to 1 week or freeze for up to 1 month.

Makes 6-8

PUMPKIN HASH BROWNS

DF GF LC NF PB* SF

If you know me well, you probably know by now that I'm obsessed with fritters, rostis and hash browns. I think they're the best way to get more veggies into your day and I simply can't resist the golden-brown crunch that comes along with them. These are a staple in my house and soon will be in yours.

250 g (2 cups) grated butternut pumpkin
3 tablespoons arrowroot or tapioca flour
1 egg, whisked
1 teaspoon chilli flakes, plus extra to
    serve if you like it spicy
1 teaspoon smoked paprika
1 teaspoon sea salt
2 tablespoons butter or coconut oil

3 tablespoons roughly chopped
    flat-leaf parsley leaves

CHUNKY LIME AVO
1 avocado, roughly diced
zest and juice of 2 limes
½ teaspoon sea salt

Preheat the oven to 120°C.

Place the pumpkin, arrowroot or tapioca flour, egg, chilli flakes, paprika and salt in a large bowl and mix well to make a thick and chunky batter.

Melt some of the butter or coconut oil in a large frying pan over medium–high heat. Add 1 heaped tablespoon of mixture per hash brown to the pan and press down gently with the back of your spoon to flatten. Cook for 4–5 minutes, or until lightly golden brown and firm enough to flip. Use a spatula to flip carefully, then press down lightly and continue to cook for 4–5 minutes, or until golden brown on both sides and cooked through. Transfer to a plate and place in the oven to keep warm. Repeat until you have eight to 10 hash browns in total.

To make the chunky lime avo, place the ingredients in a bowl and use the back of a fork to mash together until just combined. You want the avocado to be a little rough and chunky.

To serve, place your pumpkin hash browns on a share platter or serving plates, top with the chunky lime avo, chopped parsley and a sprinkle of extra chilli flakes, if desired.

Serves 2

FAKE IT!

SNACKABLE FACT
To transform these bars into choc–cherry bombs, simply roll the cherry mixture into small balls, allow them to set in the freezer, then dunk them in cooled melted chocolate.

INDULGE IT!

IT!

RICH
MIDNIGHT
SNACKS AND
DECADENT
COMFORT
FOOD

EMOTIONAL EATING

Having a healthy relationship with what we eat is especially important when it comes to managing how we use food for our mood. There is no doubt that food is nourishing on so many levels: it feeds our cells, but more than that, it fills our souls. We all have our favourite foods that put us in an awesome mood; but our mood can also have us craving our favourite foods. Moderating our relationship with food and mood is something to be mindful of, as it can be easy to slip into using foods to boost our mood, or support a low or bad mood, which is when emotional or binge eating can come into play. If you notice yourself using food, and lots of it, as an emotional crutch for what's going on inside your head and heart, be careful you don't see it as a form of therapy. If your default when you've had a rough day is to devour an entire tray of cookies, reframe your response to your emotions and find new ways to rebuild and fill your cup. I go for a walk outside, head to the gym, spend time in nature, connect with my dogs, call a loved one or meditate. Having other positive distractions can be a super helpful way to avoid using food to manage my emotions. Tune in and listen to your body and respond with love.

INDULGE IT!

ROASTED NUTS
(SWEET AND SAVOURY VERSIONS)

MEXICAN-SPICED MIXED NUTS
DF GF LC PB SF

Here, the slight kick from the Mexican-inspired spice combination is perfectly balanced by the crunchy and salty lightly roasted nuts. Mix and match using your favourite nuts.

300 g (2 cups) mixed raw nuts (I like pecans, macadamia nuts and cashew nuts)
2 tablespoons olive oil
1 teaspoon garlic powder
1 teaspoon onion powder

1 teaspoon smoked paprika
1 teaspoon cayenne pepper
1 teaspoon chilli powder
1 teaspoon sea salt
½ teaspoon ground cinnamon

Preheat the oven to 160°C and line a large baking tray with baking paper.

Combine all the ingredients in a bowl and mix well to evenly cover the nuts with all the flavours.

Spread the nut mixture out on the prepared tray and roast, stirring the nuts and turning the tray halfway through, for 15–20 minutes, or until aromatic and lightly golden brown. Keep an eye on the nuts as they roast, as ovens can differ in temperature and you don't want them to burn.

Enjoy the spiced mixed nuts warm as a snack or allow to cool on the tray, then roughly chop and stir into guacamole or sprinkle over a salad. Store in a glass jar in the pantry for up to 2 weeks or in the fridge for up to 3 months.

Makes 300 g

MAPLE–VANILLA BEAN CANDIED CASHEW CLUSTERS

DF GF LC SF

These cashew clusters provide a delicious maple-caramel crunch with every bite.

1 egg white
2 teaspoons vanilla bean paste or powder
300 g (2 cups) raw cashew nuts

70 g (½ cup) coconut sugar
3 tablespoons maple syrup
1 teaspoon ground cinnamon

Preheat the oven to 120°C and line a large baking tray with baking paper.

Whisk the egg white in a large bowl until light and frothy. Add the vanilla and whisk until well combined. Now add the cashew nuts, toss to coat well, then stir in the coconut sugar, maple syrup and cinnamon.

Spread the cashew nuts out on the prepared tray and roast, turning every 15 minutes or so, for 50–60 minutes, or until lightly golden brown and crispy.

Enjoy the candied cashew clusters warm or allow to cool on the tray, then transfer to a glass jar. Store in the pantry for up to 2 weeks or in the fridge for up to 3 months.

Makes 300 g

SNACKABLE FACT

All my sweet or savoury roasted nut recipes can be made nut free by swapping in your favourite seed combination. Roast, keeping an eye on the seeds so they don't burn, in a 160°C oven for 10–15 minutes, or until golden brown.

NO-FUSS NACHOS

DF GF LC PB SF

I am a sucker for nachos, but rather than filling up on corn chips, I reckon it's way better to swap them for a more nutrient-dense lower-carb option – because the lower the carbs the more we can eat, right?

400 g butternut pumpkin, peeled
   and deseeded
3 tablespoons extra-virgin olive oil
3 tablespoons arrowroot or tapioca flour
1 teaspoon smoked paprika
sea salt and freshly ground black pepper
3–4 tomatoes, finely diced
handful of coriander or flat-leaf parsley
   leaves, to serve

CHUNKY ZESTY AVOCADO SALSA
2 avocados, finely diced
1 tablespoon extra-virgin olive oil
   or avocado oil
1 teaspoon chilli flakes
zest and juice of 2 limes

CREAMY CASHEW CHEESE
310 g (2 cups) cashew nuts, soaked
   in boiling water for 1 hour, drained
125 ml (½ cup) filtered water
1 teaspoon sea salt
zest and juice of 1 lemon

Preheat the oven to 200°C and line two large baking trays with baking paper.

Cut your pumpkin into 3–4 mm thick slices, then cut into irregular corn chip shapes and transfer to a large bowl. Pour in the olive oil and coat well. Add the arrowroot or tapioca flour, paprika and a generous sprinkle of salt. Massage with your hands to get even coverage.

Arrange the pumpkin triangles in a single layer on the prepared trays, allowing plenty of space between each slice for maximum crispiness. Bake for 20–30 minutes, or until crispy and golden brown.

Meanwhile, place all the chunky zesty avocado salsa ingredients in a bowl and toss gently to combine.

Combine all the creamy cashew cheese ingredients in a food processor and blitz until smooth.

When ready to serve, arrange the pumpkin chips on a platter. Dollop on spoonfuls of the chunky zesty avocado salsa and creamy cashew cheese, scatter over the tomato and sprinkle on the coriander or parsley. Season well with salt and pepper and enjoy.

Serves 4

SNACKABLE FACT

You can make the chips using sweet potato, too, or try a combination of pumpkin and sweet potato. Feel free to mix it up.

MAPLE AND CINNAMON PUMPKIN AND BACON BITES

DF GF NF SF

If you haven't already realised, I am obsessed with pumpkin. It's incredibly versatile, making it perfect for so many different flavour combinations. Plus, it's a great option for those focusing on lower-carb recipes.

1 small kent pumpkin (about 1 kg), deseeded and quartered
250 g rindless streaky bacon slices
3 tablespoons extra-virgin olive oil
3 tablespoons maple syrup

4 garlic cloves, finely chopped
1 teaspoon ground cinnamon
zest and juice of 1 lemon
sea salt and freshly ground black pepper
8 lemon thyme sprigs

Preheat the oven to 180°C and line a baking tray with baking paper.

Cut each pumpkin quarter into approximately 3 cm thick wedges. Wrap each pumpkin wedge in one or two slices of bacon and transfer to the baking tray, skin-side down.

Combine the olive oil, maple syrup, garlic, cinnamon, lemon zest and juice and a generous pinch of salt and pepper in a small bowl. Whisk well, spoon over the pumpkin wedges, then top with the lemon thyme sprigs. Roast for 40–45 minutes, or until the pumpkin is golden brown and caramelised and the bacon is crispy.

Serve with a generous pinch of salt and pepper and enjoy hot out of the oven.

Serves 4

SNACKABLE FACT

When choosing bacon, always opt for free range, organic and nitrate free if possible. Every time you purchase food it's a vote with your dollar for better animal welfare and sustainable farming practices.

PERFECT PIZZA

DF GF SF

SNACKABLE FACT

The fattier the meat, the more flavour and nutrients it contains – and please make sure it's high-welfare meat, such as grass fed, free range and, if possible, organic.

I love pizza, and there is no more rewarding feeling than making your own from scratch. This base is failproof and will have you coming back for more. Try this version below and, as always, feel free to mix things up with your favourite toppings.

PIZZA CRUST

100 g (1 cup) blanched almond meal
125 g (1 cup) arrowroot or tapioca flour, plus extra for dusting
65 g (½ cup) coconut flour
1 teaspoon garlic powder
1 teaspoon onion powder
sea salt
185 ml (¾ cup) extra-virgin olive oil, plus extra for drizzling
1 tablespoon apple cider vinegar
2 eggs, at room temperature, whisked

PIZZA TOPPINGS

1 tablespoon extra-virgin olive oil or butter
2 long red chillies, finely chopped
2 garlic cloves, finely chopped
1 red onion, half finely diced, half finely sliced
300 g fatty beef, lamb or pork mince
200 g canned diced or crushed tomatoes
sea salt and freshly ground black pepper
handul of basil leaves
handul of baby rocket leaves

Preheat the oven to 220°C and line a large baking tray with baking paper.

To start on the pizza crust, combine the almond meal, arrowroot or tapioca flour, half the coconut flour, the garlic and onion powders and 1 teaspoon of salt in a large bowl and whisk well. Pour in the oil and stir to form a wet dough. Add the vinegar and egg and stir well to combine. Gradually knead in the remaining coconut flour, 1 tablespoon at a time, adding only what is needed to turn it into a thick, but slightly sticky, workable dough.

Lightly dust a clean work surface with the extra arrowroot or tapioca flour and knead and shape the dough into a 30 cm round. It'll be lovely and thin, which will help it go crispy when cooking. Transfer to the prepared tray and bake for 8–10 minutes, or until the crust is lightly golden.

Now for the toppings. Heat your preferred cooking fat in a large frying pan over medium–high heat. Add the chilli, garlic and diced onion and saute for 2–3 minutes, or until softened, golden brown and caramelised. Add the mince and cook, stirring to break up any lumps, until browned. Stir through the tomatoes and cook until the sauce thickens and becomes a little sticky.

Spread the cooked mince over the par-baked pizza crust, scatter over the finely sliced onion and season with salt and pepper. Bake for 5–6 minutes, or until the edge of your pizza is golden brown and the top of the mince is lovely and charred. (You can use the oven grill function if you like.)

To serve, top with the basil, rocket and a drizzle of extra-virgin olive oil.

Serves 4

TERRIFIC MINI CHICKEN TACOS

DF GF LC SF

SNACKABLE FACT

Most store-bought Mexican meal kits are loaded with highly refined and inflammatory oils and sugars. Always opt to make your own to improve your health.

Make it Taco Tuesday every day with this delicious and healthy recipe that shows you how quick and easy it is to make your own taco shells that are next-level tasty and crispy. Feel free to load them up with whatever fillings you like. I also love adding Mexican-style beef mince.

2 tablespoons extra-virgin olive oil or butter
1 red onion, finely chopped
3 garlic cloves, finely chopped
1 long red chilli, finely chopped
600 g chicken tenderloins
2 tablespoons Mexican seasoning mix
3 tablespoons tomato paste
125 g (½ cup) canned crushed tomatoes
sea salt and freshly ground black pepper

TACO SHELLS
2 eggs
2 tablespoons extra-virgin olive oil,
    plus extra for greasing

2 teaspoons apple cider vinegar
150 g (1½ cups) blanched almond meal
60 g (½ cup) tapioca flour
65 g (½ cup) coconut flour
1 teaspoon gluten-free baking powder
sea salt

TO SERVE
¼ iceberg lettuce, shredded
1 avocado, cut into small chunks
200 g yellow cherry tomatoes, quartered
25 g (½ cup) coriander sprigs
lime wedges

Preheat the oven to 160°C. Take a large 12-hole muffin tin, turn it upside down and grease the gaps between the moulds with olive oil. Alternatively, you can use rounds of baking paper in the gaps to support the tacos.

For the taco shells, place the eggs, olive oil and vinegar in a large bowl and whisk well. Add the almond meal, tapioca flour, coconut flour, baking powder and 1 teaspoon of salt. Beat with a hand-held mixer for 4–6 minutes, or until a firm workable dough forms. Cover and transfer to the fridge for 10 minutes to rest.

Divide the dough into eight evenly sized balls. Place each ball between two pieces of baking paper and use a rolling pin to flatten into 13 cm discs. Arrange the discs in the gaps of the prepared muffin tin and bake for 20 minutes, or until the taco shells are lightly golden brown and crispy. Set aside while you start on the filling.

Heat your preferred cooking fat in a large frying pan over medium–high heat. Add the onion, garlic and chilli and cook, stirring, for 3–4 minutes, or until softened, golden brown and caramelised. Add the chicken and seasoning mix and cook, stirring occasionally, for 4–5 minutes, or until the chicken is golden brown and the spice is well incorporated. Add the tomato paste and crushed tomatoes, season well with salt and pepper and cook for 3–4 minutes, or until the chicken is cooked through and the sauce has thickened.

To serve, load up the taco shells with the shredded iceberg, chicken, avocado, cherry tomato and coriander. Add a squeeze of lime juice and you're good to go.

Makes 8

INDULGE IT!

NICE CREAM

I scream, you scream, we all scream for NICE cream! Your tastebuds will be screaming from the rooftops when you try this one-ingredient vegan snack – sort of ice cream meets soft-serve meets gelato – that you can flavour any which way you want.

Follow the outline below and for each component feel free to use one element straight up or try a combo of a few to make your perfect blend.

When experimenting with different ingredients it's important to be intuitive. If your banana won't blend nice and smoothly, give it a few minutes to thaw slightly; if it becomes too runny, add some blend-in flavourings to thicken it up.

Depending on the combo, your nice cream can be DF, GF, LC, NF, PB or SF.

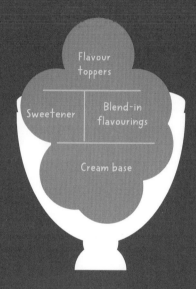

Flavour toppers

Sweetener

Blend-in flavourings

Cream base

CREAM BASE
4 cups

frozen very ripe bananas,
cut into 2 cm thick slices

SWEETENER
1 tablespoon

coconut nectar
honey
maple syrup
monk fruit syrup

BLEND-IN FLAVOURINGS
to taste

blackberries
blueberries
cacao powder
ground cinnamon
macadamia nut butter
peanut butter
raspberries
strawberries
vanilla bean paste or powder

FLAVOUR TOPPERS
(OPTIONAL)

bee pollen
cacao nibs
chocolate chunks
muesli or granola
sliced fresh fruit
toasted coconut flakes
toasted nuts

METHOD

To get started on your base, add the banana to a food processor or high-speed blender and blitz for 3–5 minutes, or until the banana is completely smooth, light and perfectly blended. Feel free to stop from time to time to scrape down the side (a tamper comes in handy if using a blender).

Once your nice cream base is at the desired consistency, add your sweetener and blend-in flavourings and blitz until just incorporated. Serve immediately as is, or add your flavour toppers and enjoy. Store in an airtight container in the freezer for up to 2 weeks.

Serves 4

TIP

For the ultimate scoopable nice cream, spoon your creation into a small loaf tin or container and transfer to the freezer for 2 hours to firm up. Scoop out when you're ready to serve. If too frozen, simply set aside at room temperature for a few minutes to soften slightly.

SELF-SAUCING SALTED CARAMEL COOKIE

GF SF

SNACKABLE FACT

Leftover caramel sauce is perfect added to smoothies or smoothie bowls or on top of your nice cream.

This recipe ain't for the faint hearted: it's rich, decadent and takes a little effort, but don't let that scare you off. Make some time on a weekend to whip this up; you will not be sorry.

270 g (1½ cups) coconut sugar
150 g (1½ cups) blanched almond meal
60 g (½ cup) arrowroot or tapioca flour
1 teaspoon gluten-free baking powder
½ teaspoon sea salt
125 g butter, melted
1 egg
1 teaspoon vanilla bean paste or powder
200 g dark chocolate (80% cacao minimum
   or to make your own, see page 40),
   broken into small chunks

SALTED CARAMEL SAUCE
500 ml (2 cups) canned coconut milk
150 g (1 cup) coconut sugar
1 teaspoon vanilla bean paste or powder
2 tablespoons coconut oil
½ teaspoon sea salt flakes

To get started, make the salted caramel sauce. Place the coconut milk, coconut sugar, vanilla, coconut oil and salt in a large saucepan over medium heat and bring to the boil. Reduce the heat to low and simmer, stirring frequently so the sauce doesn't stick to the base of the pan and burn, for 30–40 minutes, or until thick and silky. Set aside to cool and thicken.

For the cookie, in a large bowl, combine the coconut sugar, almond meal, arrowroot or tapioca flour, baking powder and salt and mix with a spoon until just combined. Add the melted butter, egg and vanilla and use a wooden spoon or spatula to mix until well incorporated.

Press half the dough into the base of a 24 cm oven-safe frying pan (I use the same pan I used to melt the butter). Make sure the dough comes up the side to cover. Fill this cavity with some of the salted caramel sauce, making sure you leave enough room for topping your cookie. Roll the remaining dough between two sheets of baking paper into a fairly even, flat disc that is 24 cm in diameter. Carefully remove the baking paper and place the disc of dough on top of the caramel layer, using your fingers to seal around the edge, then press the small chocolate chunks into the top. Transfer to the fridge to firm up for 30 minutes.

Now is a good time to preheat the oven to 180°C.

Remove the cookie from the fridge and bake for 15–20 minutes, or until cooked through and golden brown on top. Serve in the pan with a drizzle of the remaining salted caramel sauce. When you've used all you need for this recipe, pour the remaining salted caramel sauce into an airtight glass container and store in the fridge for up to 2 weeks.

Serves 8

BANGIN' BANANA POPS

DF GF PB SF

I used to love treats like this as a kid and, to be honest, nothing's changed. They're a great way to have a snack that feels a little naughty, but is a whole lot of nice.

4 large, ripe but firm bananas
80 g (½ cup) roughly chopped peanuts, toasted
10 g (½ cup) freeze-dried strawberry chunks
30 g (½ cup) shredded coconut, toasted
250 g (1 cup) melted dark chocolate (80% cacao minimum or to make your own, see opposite)

HOMEMADE CHOCOLATE (OPTIONAL)
220 g (1 cup) cacao butter
125 g (1 cup) cacao powder
125 ml (½ cup) maple syrup, honey or coconut nectar
1 teaspoon vanilla bean paste or powder

You'll need 8 wooden ice-cream sticks for this recipe.

Peel each banana, cut them in half crossways and insert an ice-cream stick into the cut end of each half. Place on a tray lined with baking paper, cover with plastic wrap and freeze for 4–6 hours, or until just frozen. You want them really cold, as this helps the chocolate to set.

If making the homemade chocolate, melt the cacao butter in a saucepan over medium–low heat. Add the cacao powder, sweetener and vanilla and whisk until smooth. Remove from the heat and set aside to thicken slightly.

Set up three shallow bowls for a dipping station. Place the peanuts in one bowl, the freeze-dried strawberry chunks in another and the toasted coconut in the third bowl.

Dip each frozen banana in the melted chocolate to cover completely, then place back on the baking paper and scatter on the toppings. You can go rough and rustic by mixing up the toppings, or make a couple of each flavour. Once you're happy with your topping decorations, return the banana pops to the freezer to set completely. They don't take long to thaw – if you let them sit at room temperature for 5 minutes or so, they'll be ready to bite into.

Makes 8

CHOC–BLUEBERRY SELF-SAUCING PUDDINGS

GF LC SF

I used to think the oozy goodness of self-saucing chocolate puddings was reserved for fine-dining restaurants. Well, breaking news: you can now create them at home, and they are next-level good.

2 tablespoons cacao powder, sifted
250 g unsalted butter, plus extra
  for greasing
200 g dark chocolate (80% cacao
  minimum or to make your own,
  see page 40), roughly chopped
125 ml (½ cup) maple syrup, coconut
  nectar or monk fruit syrup
3 eggs

3 egg yolks
1 teaspoon vanilla bean paste or powder
½ teaspoon ground cinnamon
½ teaspoon sea salt
25 g (¼ cup) blanched almond meal
1 tablespoon arrowroot or tapioca flour
125 g (½ cup) vanilla bean coconut yoghurt,
  coconut cream or ice cream
80 g (½ cup) fresh or frozen blueberries

Preheat the oven to 180°C and grease four 125 ml (½ cup) ramekins or pudding bowls with butter.

Dust inside each ramekin with the cacao powder, getting overall coverage, then tap out any excess. Place in a deep baking tray.

Melt the butter in a heatproof bowl over a saucepan of just-simmering water. (Make sure the bottom of the bowl doesn't touch the water.) Add the chocolate and stir with a metal spoon until smooth and silky. Remove the bowl from the heat and set aside.

Combine the sweetener, eggs, egg yolks, vanilla, cinnamon and salt in a large bowl. Beat with a hand-held mixer for 1–2 minutes, or until well incorporated and thickened slightly. Fold in the melted butter and chocolate mixture, almond meal and arrowroot or tapioca flour with a large metal spoon until thick and pudding-like.

Spoon the batter into the prepared ramekins or bowls, tap the bases on the benchtop to flatten the tops and bake for 8–10 minutes, or until the tops are firm and cooked but the centre is still oozy. Allow to cool slightly, 1–2 minutes max, as you don't want them to keep cooking. Use a knife to loosen each pudding from the inside edge of the ramekin or bowl, then turn out onto a serving plate. Top with the coconut yoghurt, cream or ice cream and blueberries and enjoy all that gooey chocolatey goodness.

Serves 4

SALTED PISTACHIO NICE CREAM

DF GF PB SF

I love what pistachio nuts do for recipes. Not only do they add exceptional taste and texture, but they have a unique colour you can't get from other nuts or seeds. Here, they really lend themselves to this fresh and vibrant nice cream.

4 frozen bananas, diced
500 ml (2 cups) coconut cream
2 frozen avocados, cut into chunks
90 g (2 loosely packed cups) baby
    spinach leaves
250 ml (1 cup) maple syrup, coconut
    nectar or monk fruit syrup

210 g (1½ cups) raw roughly chopped
    pistachio nuts, toasted
80 g (½ cup) raw macadamia nuts, soaked
    in boiling water for 15 minutes, drained
2 teaspoons vanilla bean paste or powder
1 teaspoon sea salt

Place the banana, coconut cream, avocado, spinach, sweetener, 65 g (½ cup) of pistachio nuts, the macadamia nuts, vanilla and salt in a food processor or high-speed blender and blitz well, scraping down the side to ensure everything is combined. (Using a tamper with a blender is handy for this.)

Stir through another 65 g (½ cup) of pistachio nuts, then transfer the mixture to a 24 cm × 13 cm loaf tin. Sprinkle over the remaining pistachios, cover with plastic wrap and place in the freezer for 3–4 hours, or until set and scoopable.

Serves 8

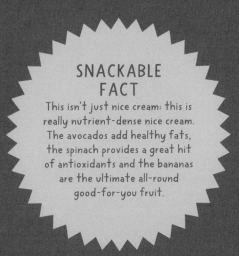

SNACKABLE FACT

This isn't just nice cream: this is really nutrient-dense nice cream. The avocados add healthy fats, the spinach provides a great hit of antioxidants and the bananas are the ultimate all-round good-for-you fruit.

INDULGE IT!

GOLDEN APPLE PIES

DF* GF LC SF

I love apple pies, they're so warming and comforting and are the best winter snack. I like to use a six-hole jumbo muffin tin, but feel free to make one large pie in a 24 cm pie dish and extend the baking time by 10–15 minutes. These are delicious served warm with a dollop of cream or your favourite nice cream.

CRUST
100 g (1 cup) blanched almond meal
60 g (½ cup) arrowroot or tapioca flour
3 tablespoons coconut flour
35 g melted butter or coconut oil
3 tablespoons maple syrup, coconut nectar
   or monk fruit syrup
½ teaspoon sea salt
1 egg

FILLING
8 granny smith apples, cored, peeled and
   cut into 5 mm cubes
zest and juice of 2 lemons
125 ml (½ cup) maple syrup, coconut nectar
   or monk fruit syrup
1 tablespoon arrowroot or tapioca flour
1 tablespoon ground cinnamon
1 teaspoon ground ginger
1 teaspoon vanilla bean paste or powder
½ teaspoon sea salt

CRUMBLE
55 g (½ cup) blanched almond meal
70 g (½ cup) coconut sugar
125 g (½ cup) softened butter, or coconut
   oil for dairy free
70 g (½ cup) roughly chopped raw
   macadamia nuts
70 g (½ cup) roughly chopped raw pecans
1 teaspoon ground cinnamon
1 teaspoon vanilla bean paste or powder

Lightly grease a six-hole jumbo muffin tin. Cut six thick strips of baking paper and lay them across each hole – these 'slings' will help lift the pies out safely.

To get started on the crust, place the almond meal, arrowroot or tapioca flour, coconut flour, butter or coconut oil, sweetener and salt in a food processor and pulse until crumbs form. Add the egg and pulse a few times to make a wet dough. Roll into a ball, flatten slightly into a disc and cover in plastic wrap. Transfer to the fridge to rest for 15 minutes.

Remove the dough from the fridge, place between two pieces of baking paper and use a rolling pin to roll into a 30 cm × 50 cm rectangle about 5 mm thick. If the dough is sticking to the paper, sprinkle over a little more arrowroot or tapioca flour to keep it workable.

Remove the top piece of baking paper and cut out six 15 cm rounds from the dough. Press the dough rounds into the prepared muffin tin, using small pieces of leftover dough to patch and fill any gaps. Transfer the tin to the fridge.

Preheat the oven to 190°C.

Combine the filling ingredients in a large bowl and mix well. Cover and transfer to the fridge.

Place the crumble ingredients in a large bowl and work with your fingers until the mixture resembles a chunky, coarse sand.

Remove the tin from the fridge and fill each crust with the filling, stopping just short of the top and leaving any excess liquid in the bowl. Scatter over the crumble, loosely cover the tin with foil and bake for 20–30 minutes. Remove the foil and bake for another 10 minutes, or until golden brown. Remove from the oven and allow to cool slightly before serving. Best enjoyed fresh, but leftovers can be stored in an airtight container in the fridge for up to 5 days.

Serves 6

MINI LEMON AND PASSIONFRUIT CHEESECAKES

GF LC* SF

If you can tolerate dairy and you're going low carb or keto, you can't go past these mini cheesecakes. They're basically tiny bite-sized versions of a baked cheesecake, meaning you can grab one and eat it on the go.

125 g (½ cup) fresh or frozen and thawed passionfruit pulp

CRUST
200 g (2 cups) blanched almond meal
70 g (½ cup) coconut sugar, or granulated monk fruit sweetener for low carb
85 g butter, melted

LEMON FILLING
250 g (1 cup) cream cheese
125 g (½ cup) sour cream, at room temperature
2 eggs, at room temperature
70 g (½ cup) coconut sugar, or granulated monk fruit sweetener for low carb
zest and juice of 2 lemons
1 teaspoon vanilla bean paste or powder

Preheat the oven to 180°C and line a 12-hole muffin tin with paper cases (or use a silicone muffin tray).

For the crust, place the almond meal, sweetener and butter in a bowl and mix well to combine.

Spoon the crust evenly into the prepared muffin tin, then use the back of the spoon to press the mixture into the base so it's packed firm. Set aside.

For the lemon filling, place all the ingredients in a large bowl and beat with a hand-held mixer until smooth and creamy.

Spoon the lemon filling over the crust and bake for 15–20 minutes, or until the cheesecakes are lightly golden brown on top and cooked through.

Allow the cheesecakes to cool slightly, then transfer to the fridge to chill for 3–4 hours, or until set.

To serve, top each cheesecake with some passionfruit pulp and enjoy.

Makes 12

CONVERSION CHARTS

Measuring cups and spoons may vary slightly from one country to another, but the difference is generally not enough to affect a recipe. All cup and spoon measures are level.

One Australian metric measuring cup holds 250 ml (8 fl oz), one Australian metric tablespoon holds 20 ml (4 teaspoons) and one Australian metric teaspoon holds 5 ml. North America, New Zealand and the UK use a 15 ml (3-teaspoon) tablespoon.

LIQUID MEASURES

One American pint = 500 ml (16 fl oz)

One Imperial pint = 600 ml (20 fl oz)

Cup	Metric	Imperial
⅛ cup	30 ml	1 fl oz
¼ cup	60 ml	2 fl oz
⅓ cup	80 ml	2½ fl oz
½ cup	125 ml	4 fl oz
⅔ cup	160 ml	5 fl oz
¾ cup	180 ml	6 fl oz
1 cup	250 ml	8 fl oz
2 cups	500 ml	16 fl oz
2¼ cups	560 ml	20 fl oz
4 cups	1 litre	32 fl oz

DRY MEASURES

The most accurate way to measure dry ingredients is to weigh them. However, if using a cup, add the ingredient loosely to the cup and level with a knife; don't compact the ingredient unless the recipe requests 'firmly packed'.

Metric	Imperial
15 g	½ oz
30 g	1 oz
60 g	2 oz
125 g	4 oz (¼ lb)
185 g	6 oz
250 g	8 oz (½ lb)
375 g	12 oz (¾ lb)
500 g	16 oz (1 lb)
1 kg	32 oz (2 lb)

LENGTH

Metric	Imperial
3 mm	⅛ inch
6 mm	¼ inch
1 cm	½ inch
2.5 cm	1 inch
5 cm	2 inches
18 cm	7 inches
20 cm	8 inches
23 cm	9 inches
25 cm	10 inches
30 cm	12 inches

OVEN TEMPERATURES

Celsius	Fahrenheit	Celsius	Gas mark
100°C	200°F	110°C	¼
120°C	250°F	130°C	½
150°C	300°F	140°C	1
160°C	325°F	150°C	2
180°C	350°F	170°C	3
200°C	400°F	180°C	4
220°C	425°F	190°C	5
		200°C	6
		220°C	7
		230°C	8
		240°C	9
		250°C	10

THANKS

Rob Palmer
An absolute joy and pleasure to finally work with you, mate. The combination of your incredible talent, eye for detail and love for what you do was only matched by your enthusiasm, good vibes and can-do attitude. Love your work!

Berni Smithies
You are an absolute gem, Berni. I am so grateful for the way you worked on this book, with a level of precision, care and love as if it were your own. I loved watching you turn my recipes into something beyond what I could have asked for. Keep shining.

Naomi van Groll
From that first Friday we got stuck into the shoot, I just knew you and I were on the same page. With a contagiously positive energy and passion for creating a beautiful book, your smile lit up the room and kept us going. Thank you.

Kerrie Ray
Dog people really are the best kind of people. Once I heard you were a fellow animal lover, I knew we would get along really well, but once you started cooking with such care and love, I knew we'd make a dream team on the tools! You rock!

Sandy Goh
Sandy, you're the ultimate kitchen companion. You get what needs to be done with such care, grace and precision that I can't imagine having made this book without you. Your contagious, fun and easy-going energy brightened my days!

Mark Roper
Our seventh book together, legend! We must be doing something right, huh?! I know what you are doing right, though: bringing your A-game, as always. Thanks for smashing it out of the park! You're so good, it's a privilege to ride this wave with you.

Deb Kaloper
You're so intuitive, I feel like you and I can talk without saying a word and understand what the other is thinking and feeling. It's so powerful on a shoot, where we work together so closely. You bring such an amazing tenderness and care to my books that I am so grateful for.

Caroline Griffiths
When my recipes are in your hands I have the ultimate peace of mind because you just get it. You get me, my style and what we want from the book, and that is priceless. Thanks for your love and care in making every dish jump off the page with yum.

Sarah Watson
Working with you is like working with a best friend I haven't seen in years, in that I always feel like you've got my back in making sure everything we do is mindful and meaningful. So grateful to have you as part of another wonderful book, thank you for bringing your best as always.

Megan Johnston
Thanks for making the first of what I hope is to be many more times working together so incredibly seamless, fun and precise. It was such a breeze working with you, and your eye for detail has really elevated this book to where it is now. Thank you for looking after my words so well.

Andy Warren
Wow, wow, wow. Andy. You know how to put my energy on a page. And not just one page, but all 192 of them! You've brought this book not only to life, but thrust it out of this universe with its positivity and contagiously fun energy from start to finish. Thanks, legend!

Clare Marshall
Clare, I could gush for pages and pages about what a joy it was to work so closely with you on this beautiful book. But because you did such an incredible job, we actually don't have any more space, so I'll just say this. Positive, fun, open, caring, giving and so damn talented. Thank you for being an absolute joy to work with.

Mary Small
What can I say, Mary Small?! This is no ordinary book. Two states, two shoots, two teams, but despite the adventure getting it done, it was surrounded by a whole lotta love! Thank you for really sticking by this beautiful book with BIG personality! It was SO worth it and I am so proud to be published by you and the wonderful team at Plum, which surrounds my books with so much support, guidance and love. Thanks for believing in me.

INDEX

C

Pan Macmillan acknowledges the Traditional Custodians of Country throughout Australia and their connections to lands, waters and communities. We pay our respect to Elders past and present and extend that respect to all Aboriginal and Torres Strait Islander peoples today. We honour more than sixty thousand years of storytelling, art and culture.

A Plum book
First published in 2021 by
Pan Macmillan Australia Pty Limited
Level 25, 1 Market Street,
Sydney, NSW 2000, Australia

Level 3, 112 Wellington Parade,
East Melbourne, VIC 3002, Australia

Design by Andy Warren
Edited by Megan Johnston
Index by Helena Holmgren
Photography by Rob Palmer and Mark Roper
Food and prop styling by Deborah Kaloper and Berni Smithies
Food preparation by Caroline Griffiths, Sandy Goh, Luke Hines, Kerrie Ray
  and Sarah Watson
Typeset by Megan Ellis
Colour reproduction by Splitting Image Colour Studio
Printed and bound in China by Imago Printing International Limited

A CIP catalogue record for this book is available from the National Library of Australia.

10 9 8 7 6 5 4 3 2 1